Candle
CREATIONS

Ideas for Decoration and Display

Vivian Peritts

Published by

krause publications

700 East State Street • Iola, WI 54990-0001
715/445-2214 • FAX: 715/445-4087   www.krause.com

Please call or write for our free catalog of publications. Our toll-free number to place an order or obtain a free catalog is 800-258-0929 or please use our regular business telephone 715-445-2214.

Library of Congress Catalog Number 2001088100
ISBN 0-87349-246-1

Acknowledgment

I want to thank my parents, George and Rosalie Brown, for instilling in me the creative spirit and for encouraging me to pursue my desire to "make things."

I also want to thank my husband, Virgil, for his love and never-ending support of all my projects. I thank my son, Forrest, for his good-natured approach in stepping over, not sitting on, and putting up with candles on every flat surface in the house while I worked on this book.

I could not have written this book without the faithful help of Paula Heiney on the computer. Not only can she read my writing, but she knows what I'm trying to say no matter how I spell it. I also had a lot of help from my friend Linda Baird in meeting my delivery deadlines.

I want to thank Colonial Candle of Cape Cod for the majority of the candles that you see in this book and to all the suppliers mentioned in the resource guide at the end of the book. Thanks to all of the companies for making the wonderful products that were sent to help make all these projects.

I need to thank the power company for keeping the power on during the many snowstorms we had while I was writing this book. So no one had to light my candles before the book was finished!!

Many thanks to Krause Publications for giving me the opportunity to write this book, and especially Brian Earnest.

Most of all, I thank God for the gifts of imagination and creativity. He also gave me the ability to turn them into beautiful projects that I can share with others. I have thoroughly enjoyed this adventure!

Preface

This is not a book on how to make candles. It is a book about how to take plain store-bought candles and turn them into your own unique creations. All this you can do in less than half the time it would take you to make them from scratch.

But remember that crafting the candles is only part of the story; presentation is what completes the tale. The candleholder is just as important as the candle and completes the look. Displaying your completed candles and candleholders will have your guests in awe of your decorating talents.

Introduction

Candles, candles and more candles. I love them, but because I learned several lessons the hard way, let's say the messy way, I am no longer allowed to make my candle creations in the kitchen! I am now resigned to using a hot plate in the basement. Please read all the instructions carefully so that you won't be banished from your kitchen. I have learned to follow a few simple rules and your candle crafting will be much more enjoyable if you do, too.

Basic Rules For Candle Crafting:

1. Never wear your good clothes or your favorite shoes while working with wax. You're just asking for trouble if you do.

2. Lay newspaper everywhere!!!!

3. Be sure that you understand the facts about displacement in the basic techniques section.

4. Never use plastic containers, or containers that leak, for melting wax.

5. Never leave your work area unattended.

Table of Contents

Chapter 1

Equipment

Heat source: You will need a kitchen stove or hot plate. If you are using a hot plate, place a tempered glass sheet (the kind sold as a cutting board) between the hot plate and your table or work surface.

Work surface: Cover the area around your heat source with layers of newspaper. Don't forget to cover the floor around your work area, especially if it's carpet! Newspaper absorbs wax and will make it easy to clean up. It's always nice not to have to scrape spilled wax off your counter top or floor. Your work area should be a stable surface. You want to avoid tables with spindly legs that will cause spills when kicked. Remember that your work surface should be out of the reach of pets and children.

Cooking pots: The safest way to heat wax is over water. Use a double boiler for melting the wax. It should be made of stainless steel or aluminum. Wax will accumulate on these pots as you use them, so don't use your good cooking pots. You can visit your local second-hand store and pick up a few large pots for pennies. Use these as the bottom of your double boiler. A container inside a container can easily be substituted for a double boiler. If you do not have a dipping vat (these are available from candle-making suppliers) use a tall tin can, or a tall galvanized French floral pot.

Trivet: Place a trivet between the two pots. This can be a jar lid, cooking rack, or a metal chain. This keeps the inside pot from touching the outside pot.

Potholders: Need we say more! Use old ones.

Thermometer: Candle-making or candy-making thermometers are the best. A candle maker's thermometer has markings for specific temperatures for dipping techniques. It should cover 38 to 108°C and 100 to 225°F.

Stirrers: Wooden spoons and wooden or metal skewers work well to stir the wax.

Pliers: Needle nose or other types of pliers can be used to grasp the wick when dipping the candle.

Hammer: This is used to break up large blocks of wax.

Wicking needle: Needles used to insert wicks.

Blow dryer: These are used to keep wax sheets pliable and candles soft while they are being manipulated.

Microwave: Used to soften pre-made candles for manipulation.

Freezer or wax paper: Has a special coating that doesn't absorb the wax so it's a good surface on which to place your freshly dipped candle.

Pitcher: Used to add water to double boiler. Since water evaporates, you need to keep replacing it.

Chapter 2

Materials

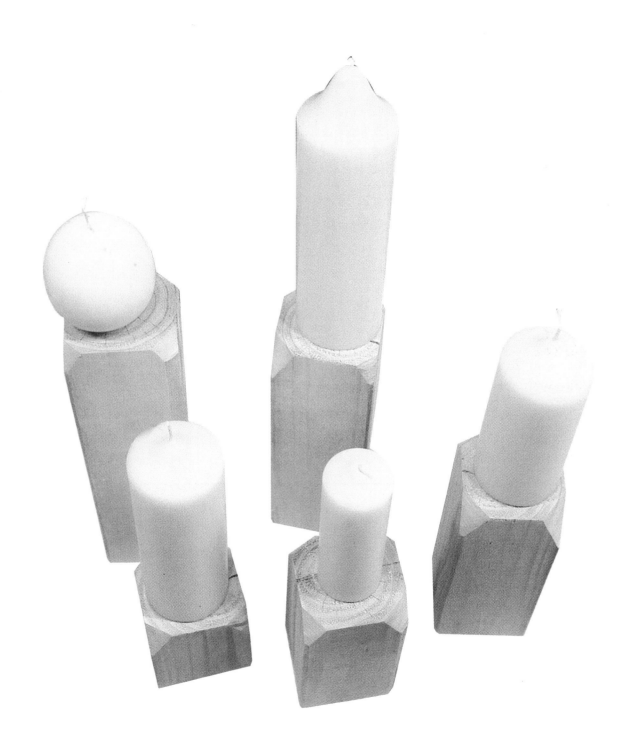

Wax: The following types can be found in craft stores.

- **Paraffin:** This is a general-purpose wax and is sold in pellets or slabs. Paraffin is usually white when solid and becomes clear and colorless when melted. It hardens with a glossy, translucent finish. Paraffin has a melting point of 140°-145°F (60°-63°C).

- **Beeswax:** Can be combined with other waxes to increase burning time.

- **Sheet wax:** Comes in a wide range of colors. The sheet can be rolled or cut into shapes called appliqués to add to candles.

Dyes: Sold in concentrated colored wax squares that can be added to melted wax. A little goes a long way, so add a quarter of a square at a time. Colors can be mixed. The wax color changes as it cools, becoming lighter and more opaque.

Mold seal: Putty used to seal the mold so that it is watertight. It can be reused.

Candle paints: There are several products in the craft store that can be combined with acrylic paint and applied to candles. There are also paints made specifically for painting on candles. They are available in jars or sprays.

Wicks: Made from plaited cotton and treated with a chemical to help them burn. It is important to use the correct size of wick. Sizes range from 1 to 10 cm (1/2" – 4"). The measurement refers to the candle size (diameter) appropriate for each wick. Wicks need to be primed before using (see Chapter 4 for directions). Primed wicks are also available in your craft store.

Adhesives: Hot glue is not a good choice. Think about it!

Wax glue: For applying wax to wax.

Glass and bead adhesive: Used for applying slick surfaces to each other or to candles (flat marbles, rocks, wire, etc.).

Double-sided adhesive: Thin sheet of adhesive covered with protective paper on both sides. Types include: PeelnStick for applying flat items to candles, and Red Liner industrial strength for applying weighty items, such as beads, to candles.

Tacky glue: Thick, white glue that dries clear and is used to adhere fiber items to candles.

Candle Definitions

Certain terms will be used throughout the book to describe the purchased candles all the projects start with. Here are the types of candles that will be used:

1 taper
2 classic (molded) taper
3 ball candle
4 votive
5 tea light
6 storm candle
7 crayon-topped pillar
8 assorted pillar

Chapter 3

Safety and Clean-up

Safety First!

Be sure that your heat source is on a stable surface. Never heat directly on top of the heat source, always use a double boiler.

Wax is flammable. If a fire breaks out while you are working don't try to put it out with water. Turn off the heat source, cover the pot with a lid, use baking soda or use a fire extinguisher. Remember to have a fire extinguisher near your work area at all times.

Have cool water standing by in case you ever have a wax burn. If burned, submerge your skin into the water (not ice water) until the wax is cool enough to remove. Keep the skin cool.

Use potholders and have a firm grip on the pot when pouring the hot wax.
When dipping a candle, always check to make sure that the wick is secure in the candle. Some wicks are added after the candle is made and are not secure.

Never leave burning candles unattended.

Clean-up

If you cover your work area and the floor around it with several layers of newspapers, clean up will be quick and easy. If not, you will have to learn to enjoy scraping wax off your counter top and floor with a spatula and a warm rag.

Remember to wear old clothes and shoes.

Containers should be ones that you keep just for candle making. If you need to remove the wax buildup or dispose of wax, then heat the container and the softened wax scum should wipe off with a paper towel.

Never pour wax down the drain. Pour it into a container that can be thrown away.

You can always save wax for the next time or make candles such as the coffee cup candle or stacked candle and just use it up.

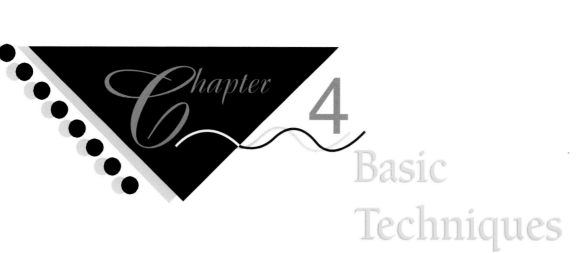

Chapter 4

Basic Techniques

Melting wax

Use a double boiler (see Chapter 1).

Water level

The water in the bottom pan of the double boiler should be deep enough to come at least halfway up the sides of the melting pot.

Temperature

Wax needs to be between 160° and 180° for overdipping candles. Hot white wax will look crystal clear in the pot. The wax clouds as it cools and finally becomes opaque when completely cool.

Dipping wax

White dipping wax is referred to quite often in this book. Premium taper wax is a good wax for dipping.

To dip a candle, hold it by its wick with a good pair of pliers (ones with ridges that can hold the wick securely) and lower the candle into the container. Candles can also be dipped by holding the bottom with your fingers.

The size of the container used for dipping is very important. It must be tall enough to accommodate the candle.

Displacement

This is very important. How much wax do you need for dipping? Too much wax can spell "disaster, mess, oops, ouch," and a few words that I won't mention. To find out how much wax is needed in your container:
• Place the candle inside the empty container and fill the container with water to just over the top of the candle.
• Remove the candle and mark the water line on the container with a permanent marker.
• Dry the inside of the container and melt enough wax to reach the marked line.

Softening candles

Several of the projects in this book require that the candle surface be softened. The method used depends on how soft the candle needs to be before the technique can be completed. I soften candles in three different ways:

Microwave oven — Place a folded paper towel in the microwave. Lay the candle on the towel and heat for the time specified in the directions.

Blow dryer — Use to warm wax sheet.

Heat gun — To melt the wax on the surface of the candle to expose embedded items such as shells or marbles.

Leveling the bottom of the candle

If after the process of working on a candle, it no longer stands straight, this is what I do to level out the situation. This is a problem that occurs only with the larger candles.

1. Line a skillet with aluminum foil and place it on a heating element. Heat the skillet on low.

2. Set the bottom of candle on the foil and move it in a circular motion. Hold the candle straight and as the wax melts the candle will level out. Remove candle and test on a flat surface.

3. Repeat if the candle is still not level.

Preparing a wick

You can buy prepared candlewicks in different lengths from any candle supplier. You can also buy wicks by the spool. The spool wicks need to be prepared before they are used. Cut the length of wick that you need for your project, dip it three or four times in the dipping wax, and lay it straight to cool.

Use a wicking needle to add the wick to the candle or just thread the stiff wick through the candle by itself.

Candlewick holder tabs can be purchased and are added to the bottom of wicks to hold them in place. Pliers can be used to crimp the prongs of the tabs around the wick. The tabs usually have outside prongs that can be pushed into the bottom of the candle.

Color

There are endless possibilities when dipping candles for color. The more times a candle is dipped in the colored wax, the more intense the color becomes.

Adding color to wax

Start with hot, white dipping wax and gradually add dye. Dipping a candle several times will also increase the intensity of the color. Check the color as you go. One way to do this is by dipping the end of a white taper into the wax as color is added. Use a color chart for mixing colors. Combining too many colors in the same batch will result in a muddy-colored wax.

Gradation

Many of the candles in this book have been dyed using this technique.

Add the color to the hot wax and proceed with one of the following variations:

Dipping the entire candle

1. Hold the candle by the wick and dip the complete candle into the dyed dipping wax. Dip as many times as you would like, keeping in mind that the color becomes more intense with every dip.

Light to dark gradations

2. Follow the directions in step one except every time you dip the candle into the dyed dipping wax; dip a little less of the candle into the wax. The results will be a graduation of color from light to dark. The bottom of the candle will be the darkest and the top will be the lightest.

Dark to light gradations

3. Follow the directions in step two, except hold the candle by the bottom with your hand. This will produce the darkest color at the top and the lightest at the bottom.

Gradation with half dip

4. Choose to follow the directions in either step or step two, but dip only half of the candle and leave the other half its original color.

Dipping at an angle

5. Choose to follow either step one or step two, but when dipping the candle hold it at an angle. You can change the angle every time you dip the candle if you prefer. This method allows for a lot of creativity in color.

Whipped wax

Wax whipping requires an electric mixer. Heat the wax first and then pour it into a large bowl. Let the wax cool until it appears cloudy. Use a piece of waxed paper over the top of the bowl and cut a slit in it for the mixer blades to fit. This will prevent splatters. Whip the wax on "high" until it is frothy and forms peaks.

Use a spatula or fork to apply the whipped wax to your candle. Pull the soft wax from the beaters and then run them under hot water to clean them. Any leftover whipped wax can be melted and reused.

Reshaping Tapers

Preparing the Candle for Manipulation

Several of these techniques are done with tapers that have just been dipped because they are still soft and easy to reshape. When starting with a store-bought taper, it must be softened first. I use my microwave oven.

Fold a clean paper towel once and lay it in the microwave. Lay the taper on the towel and set the microwave on "high" for 10 minutes. Every few minutes, turn the candle and test to see if it is flexible. A taper usually takes eight to 10 minutes to become soft and flexible (but not melting). Dip the candle in dipping wax six times with about 30 seconds between dips, then proceed immediately with the techniques below.

It is important to hang a newly reshaped taper to cool. I use a wire-hanging basket and spring clothes pins. I hang the candle on the basket by its wick and secure with a clothespin.

A candle that has been reshaped can be left as is or further decorated by painting or overdipping in color.

Twisted Tapers

Materials:
- One taper with the color throughout (12" is a good size)
- Microwave oven
- Paper towels
- Rolling pin
- Knife
- White dipping wax
- Needle-nose pliers

Instructions

1. Place the taper on a paper towel in the microwave and heat for 10 minutes on "high." Check the candle about every two minutes and turn it over on the paper. The candle is ready when it is bendable, but not melting.
2. Remove candle from the microwave and immediately dip it five times in the dipping wax. Wait 15 to 20 seconds between dips.
3. Lay the taper on a clean, smooth surface, such as a counter top.
4. Cut 1" of the wax off of the top of the candle. Be careful not to cut wick. Shape the top slightly.
5. Roll gently with a rolling pin from the top to within an inch of the bottom of the candle. If the candle sticks to the rolling pin it is too hot to roll. Wait 30 seconds and try again. Stop when the candle is flat and approximately 1/4" thick. If the candle cracks, dip again and start over.
6. Hold the top and the bottom of the candle and gently twist in opposite directions. If the candle begins to crack, dip again.
7. After the twist is complete, overdip three times.
8. Hang the candle by the wick to harden.

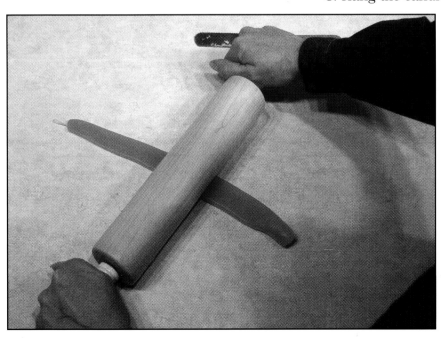

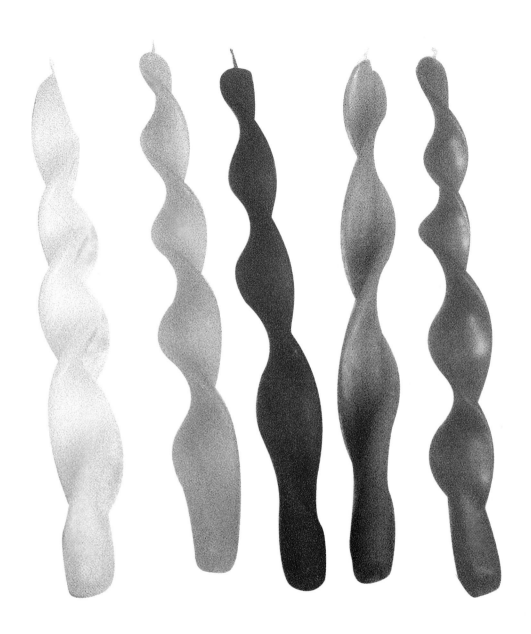

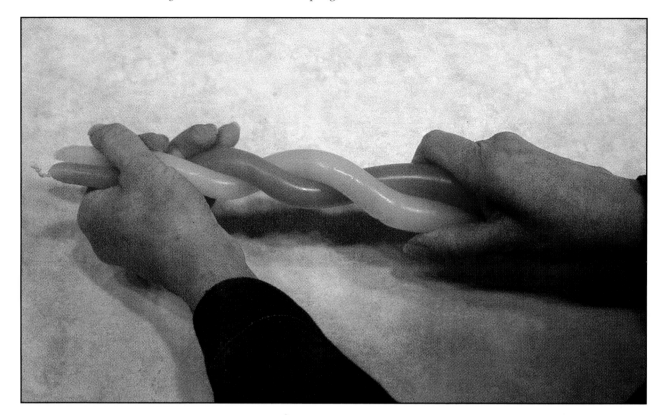

Two Tapers Twisted Together

Prepare two candles in the microwave oven at the same time. They may require a few more minutes to soften. Check the candles about every two minutes and turn them over on the paper towel. They are ready when they are bendable, but not melting.

Hold the tops of both candles with one hand and the bottoms with the other. Twist your hands in opposite directions and squeeze the bottom of the candles together to form one base. Shave the bottom of the candle with a knife or vegetable peeler to fit into the candleholder.

Half-Twisted Taper

Roll only the middle third of the prepared candle and twist. The candle will be round on the top and the bottom and twisted in the center.

Half-Dipped Twisted Taper

After twisting, dip the candle in colored wax only half way.

Chapter 6

Painted Candles

andles should be prepared before painting by cleaning them with rubbing alcohol. This will remove dirt and dust or any residue that would prevent the paint from adhering to the candle. Several products are made specifically for painting on candles. There are spray paints for candles in silver, gold, and pearl. Several paint companies make candle paint or have a candle painting medium that can be mixed with acrylic paint to make the paint adhere to the wax. This type of product makes it possible to paint your candles any color, as acrylic paints come in every color imaginable. Always follow the manufacturer's directions for mixing and application.

Silver Metallic Taper with Black Flames

Materials:
- 12" silver metallic taper
- Acrylic paint — black
- Candle painting medium
- #2 liner brush

Instructions:
1. Mix one part black paint with one part candle medium.
2. Paint wavy flames on the bottom half of the candle.

Gold Metallic Taper with Black Dots

Materials:
- 12" gold metallic taper
- Acrylic paint — black
- Round stencil sponge
- Candle painting medium

Instructions:
1. Mix equal parts of black paint and candle medium.
2. Dip the end of the stencil sponge into the paint mixture and use it to make black dots on the candle.

Candleholder:
Wrought-iron candleholder to accent the colors in the candles.

Green Metallic Taper with Dimensional Copper Dots

Materials:
- 12" green metallic taper
- Copper dimensional paint with a fine tip

Instructions:
1. Use the paint to make dimensional dots all over taper.

Opalescent Glitter Dot Tapers

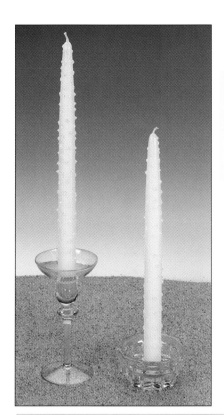

Materials:
- Two white tapers, any height
- White iris glitter dimensional paint
- Micro-fine sprinkle-on glitter

Instructions:
1. Make dots on the candle with the paint.
2. While the paint is still wet, sprinkle with glitter.

Four Painted Candles with Bead-Trimmed Candelabra

The following four candles are simple, fast and they look great together.

Materials:
- Classic-style taper — 9" tall, one each color: medium green, medium pink, butterscotch, and medium blue
- Candle painting medium
- Metal paint — bright orange, bright lime green, and strawberry
- Turquoise dimensional paint
- 3/4" masking tape
- Sea sponge
- #2 liner brush
- Pencil eraser

Instructions:

Green Candle
1. Use masking tape to tape off stripes. Leave 3/4" space between tape sections.
2. Mix equal parts candle painting medium with orange paint and sponge the exposed areas of the candle. Do not paint the top or bottom.
3. Remove tape.

Pink Candle
1. Mix equal parts candle painting medium with green paint. Use the liner brush to paint swirl design on candle.

Blue Candle
1. Mix equal parts candle painting medium with pink paint. Use the pencil eraser to make pink dots all over the candle.

Butterscotch Candle
1. Use the turquoise dimensional paint to make wavy lines down the candle.

Candleholder:
(Holds four candles) Paint an old, brass candelabra with ivory metal paint. Glue beaded fringe around each candleholder below the lip.

Green Candle

25

Baseball Candle

Materials:
- 2.8" white ball candle
- Acrylic paint — black and red
- White dipping wax
- #0 liner brush
- 1/2" x 4" piece of emery board

Instructions:

1. Draw a circle on each side of the candle. Only draw the top 3/4 of the circle. At the bottom of the circle, go down to the bottom of the candle to form the stitch line of the ball.
2. Use the liner brush and black paint to paint the stitch line.
3. To make the red stitches, cut one end of the emery board straight. Dip the cut end in the red paint and use it to make 1/2" stitches along the black lines.

Candleholder:
Displayed on a vintage metal roller skate

Cheese Candle

Materials:

- 3" x 8" triangular ivory candle
- Acrylic paint — black and antique gold
- Assorted corks for painting holes
- White dipping wax

Instructions:

1. Use the large end of the cork dipped in the black paint to paint holes in the cheese. Move the cork around on the surface of the candle to elongate the holes. Let the paint dry completely.
2. Use the small end of the cork dipped in gold to paint the center of the holes. The black should show slightly all around the edge of the gold to give dimension to the holes. Let dry completely.
3. Dip the candle in the dipping wax several times.

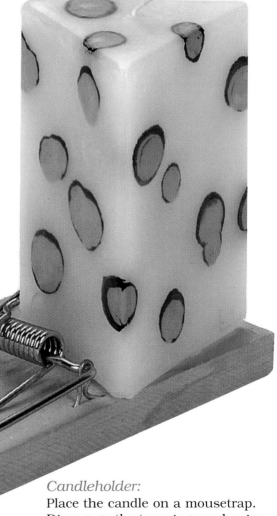

Candleholder:

Place the candle on a mousetrap. Disengage the trapping mechanism and place the candle on top of the trap.

Brown Swirl Paint Candle

Materials:
- 3" x 12" butterscotch-colored candle
- Acrylic paint — antique maroon
- Polyurethane varnish-gloss
- Size 4 fan paintbrush
- Paper plate

Instructions:
1. Place the paint on a paper plate.
2. Stick fan brush in paint and dab off excess.
3. Place the brush on the candle and make a twist with the handle, turning the brush in a circle. This creates a circular pattern.
4. Repeat this pattern over the candle. Let dry completely.
5. Coat the candle with polyurethane.

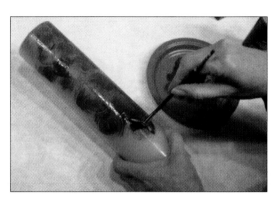

Crackle Butterfly Candle

Materials:
- 3" x 9" brown candle
- Anita's 'Fragile Crackle' Kit
- Acrylic paint — burnt umber and buttermilk
- Candle painting medium
- Polyurethane varnish-gloss
- Butterfly wallpaper border
- Glazing medium — clear art glaze
- Rags

Instructions:
1. Combine the buttermilk paint with the candle painting medium. Paint the candle and let dry.
2. Follow the instructions on the crackle medium and apply to the candle.
3. After crackle procedure is complete, mix equal parts of burnt umber and faux glaze. Paint mixture on candle. Immediately wipe off excess with rag, leaving paint in cracks. Let dry completely.
4. Seal with the varnish.
5. Select butterfly from border and cut it out.
6. Apply the butterfly to the front of the candle (see wallpaper section of Chapter 7 for complete instructions).

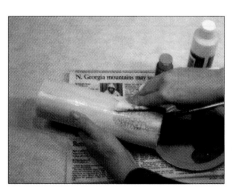

Rubber Stamping on Candles

Rubber stamping is a great way to add a design and color to your candles. Pick a stamp that will conform to the shape and size of the candle you are using. You can roll the stamp around the candle, however, the combination of the slick paint and the candle make a large stamp difficult to control.

Use the acrylic paint on the stamp. Lightly dab the paint onto the stamp with the side of a foam brush. It dries faster than stamping ink, so apply it immediately.

Fern Rubber Stamped Candles

Materials:
- 3" x 3" yellow candle
- Monkey paw fern stamp
- 1 1/2" foam brush
- Acrylic paint — pewter
- White dipping wax

Candleholder:
Displayed on an old silver bracelet

Instructions:
1. Dab paint lightly onto stamp with foam brush.
2. Apply stamp to candle by rolling the stamp across the candle. If stamping several times, reapply paint as needed.
3. Dip once in dipping wax.

Encaustic Painting

Materials:
- 3" x 9" lavender candle
- Utility candle and holder (used to melt crayon)
- Corrugated paper — dark green
- Multi-colored tiny spring clothespins
- Large tuna can

Instructions:
1. Choose a design (I used a free-form floral design). The crayons make a wide mark similar to a large-tip permanent marker, so use a simple design without fine details.
2. Remove the paper from the crayons.
3. Hold the crayon in the utility candle's flame. Immediately apply the crayon to the lavender candle. Don't leave the crayon in the flame too long or soot will cover the tip and your design will be dingy looking.

Candleholder:
1. Cover sides of large tuna can with dark green corrugated paper.
2. Cut a circle out of corrugated paper 1/2" larger than the top of the can.
4. Clip clothespins every 1/2" around the edge of the circle.
3. Glue on top of can.

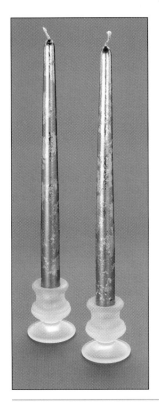

Gold Leaf Taper

Materials:
- Gold metallic taper
- Gold leaf kit (including leaf, sizing and sealer) from Houston Art, Inc.
- Sea sponge
- Soft paintbrush

Instructions:
1. Sponge sizing on candles. Do not cover completely.
2. Read kit instructions for specifics on leafing. Apply gold leaf to candle.
3. Use soft brush to remove excess gold leaf.
4. Apply sealer.

Red Candle with Gold Leaf

Materials:
- Red pillar candle
- Gold leaf kit (including leaf, sizing and sealer)
- Sea sponge
- Soft paintbrush

Instructions:
1. Follow steps 1 through 4 for gold leaf taper.
2. While sealer is still wet, roll candle in gold leaf crumbs that were brushed off previous projects. Let dry completely.
3. Apply second coat of sealer.

Paper and Candles

Decoupage

Wallpaper

Wallpaper comes plain or pre-pasted. If your wallpaper is plain you need to apply a decoupage medium or tacky glue to the wrong side before applying it to a candle. If you have pre-pasted wallpaper, after cutting your design you will need to "book it." This means you will need to wet it thoroughly, fold the wrong sides together and let it sit about five minutes. This allows the glue to activate so that the paper can be applied.

Square Ivory Candle

Materials:
- 4" x 4" x 4" ivory candle
- 4 wallpaper design cutouts trimmed to fit sides of candle
- Scissors
- Tacky glue or double-sided adhesive
- White dipping wax

Instructions:
1. Cut wallpaper design to size and prepare for application.
2. Apply to candle and wipe off excess glue. Let dry and dip once or twice into dipping wax.
3. If using double-sided adhesive, apply to candle and dip once or twice into dipping wax.
4. If using tacky glue, spread glue lightly and apply to candle, let dry. Dip candle once or twice into dipping wax.

Candleholder:
Square glass-cobbled frame with glass and backing removed.

Silver Frame Photo Candle

Materials:
- Color copies of old photos
- 3" x 6" ivory candle
- Inexpensive lightweight photo frames that can be bent to the curve of the candle
- Double-sided adhesive — cut the size of the photos
- White dipping wax
- Tacky glue

Instructions:
1. Apply double-sided adhesive to the back of the photocopies.
2. Cut out photocopies and apply to the candle.
3. Dip the candle twice in dipping wax.
4. Bend the frames to the shape of the candle.
5. Glue frame to the candle.

Candleholder:
Simple ivory dessert plate

Materials:

- 3" x 11" white pillar candle
- Wedding invitation or copy
- Double-sided adhesive
- 6" wire wreath form
- 6" circle of dark mat board (black or green)
- 3" circle of dark mat board (black or green)
- Approximately 48 paper ivy leaves with wires attached ranging from 1 1/2" to 2 1/2" lengths
- 18" multi-strand (10 to 12 strands) spray of pearls spaced on monofilament thread
- Package of monofilment loop with spaced pearls
- One gold ribbon rose
- White dipping wax
- Tacky glue

Instructions:

1. Apply double-sided adhesive to the back of the invitation. Apply to the candle about 2" down from the top.
2. Cover the wire wreath with the ivy leaves. Start around the outside edge and use the wire stems to attach the leaves. Build inward rows of leaves.
3. Glue the wire wreath to the large mat board circle. Glue the small circle inside the wreath on top of the large mat board.
4. Glue the head of the 18" pearl spray under the leaves near the inside circle of the wreath. Coil the length around the inside circle of the wreath and use a wire to attach it to the beginning of the spray forming a circle of beads.
5. The monofilament bead loops come with three loops of beaded thread on a wire stem. Remove the stems from three of the picks, leaving just enough to hold the loops in shape. Glue two of the loops to sides above the invitation and one loop headed down over the invitation. Glue only the stem section. Glue a gold rose over where the three meet.
6. Wire in three of the pearl loop picks at the meeting point of the circle of beads. The loops should stand up in the front of the candle.
7. Place the candle in the center of the wreath.

Candleholder:
The candle and wreath were placed on a short, wide, pillar-candle-size brass candlestick.

Silver and White Wedding Invitation Candle

Mr. and Mrs. Timothy Shore
request the honour of your presence
at the marriage of their daughter
Jennifer Alexandra
to
Mr. Richard Samuel Jameson
Saturday, the ninth of October
Two thousand and one
a half after six o'clock in the evening
Saint Paul's Cathedral
Baltimore, Maryland

Materials:
- 4" x 9" pillar white candle
- Invitation or a color copy of one
- Silver metallic paper cut 1" larger than invitation
- Double-sided adhesive cut the size of the invitation and silver paper
- White dipping wax
- Antique luggage tag ornament decoration by Supreme Sales
- Tacky glue

Candleholder:
Fluted glass taper holder turned upside down.

Instructions:
1. Apply the double-sided adhesive to the back of the invitation and the silver paper.
2. Trim the invitation and apply it to center of the silver paper.
3. Trim the silver paper 1/4" larger than the invitation on all sides. Apply to the candle.
4. Dip the candle twice in the dipping wax.
5. Glue on ornaments.

Giraffe Print Candle

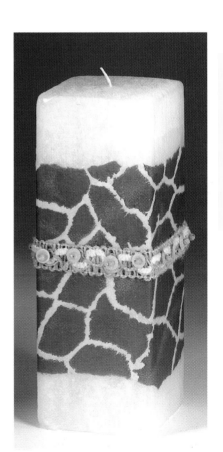

Materials
- 3" x 8" rectangular white candle
- 12 1/2" x 7" giraffe print paper
- 12 1/2" braid and button trim 1/2" wide
- 12 1/2" x 7" sheet double-sided adhesive
- Tacky glue
- White dipping wax

Instructions
1. Back giraffe paper with double-sided adhesive. Tear to give uneven edges along top and bottom of its 12 1/2" length.
2. Peel off the backing from the adhesive and apply around the middle of the candle.
3. Dip the candle twice in the dipping wax.
4. Glue the button trim around the middle of the candle.

Materials:
- 3" x 6" ivory pillar candle
- 10" x 6" Orient express paper
- Decoupage medium
- White dipping wax

Instructions:
1. Use the decoupage medium to apply the paper to the candle.
2. Dip the candle twice in the dipping wax.

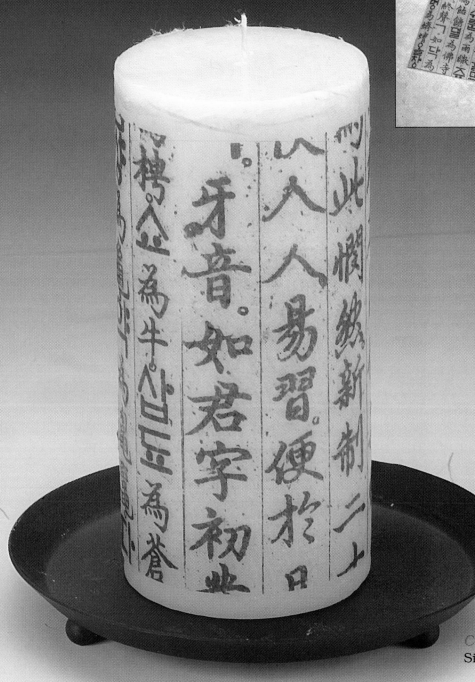

Candleholder:
Simple black candle saucer

Zebra Print Candle

Materials:
- 2" x 9" white candle
- 8" x 9" sheet of zebra-print paper
- 8" x 9" double-sided adhesive
- White dipping wax

Instructions
1. Apply the adhesive to the back of the zebra paper.
2. Remove protective paper and apply zebra paper to candle.
3. Dip the candle twice in the dipping wax.

Candleholder:
Displayed on a black-footed platform wrapped with 3 yards of 16-gauge black wire. The middle of the three yards of wire is wrapped around a river rock and the wire ends are wrapped around the candle stand.

Red and White Round Candles with Gold Decorations

Materials:
- 2.8" red ball candle
- 2.8" white ball candle
- Two gold doilies
- Tacky glue
- Small scissors

Instructions
1. Use scissors to cut between designs on doilies, separating into small patterns.
2. Use tacky glue to apply the patterns to the ornaments.

Candleholder:
Small, copper, cookie cutters with doily backing are good for displaying round ornamental candles.

Vellum Gingko Leaf Candle

Materials:
- Six vellum gingko leaves
- 3" x 6" light-green pillar candle
- White dipping wax
- One sheet double-sided adhesive
- One sheet tracing paper

Instructions
1. Remove backing from the double-sided adhesive and lay the leaves right side up on the sticky surface. They should not touch or overlap.
2. Place the tracing paper on top.
3. Use the scissors to cut as close to the leaves as possible. The tracing paper will make the cutting easier because the adhesive won't stick to the scissors.
4. Remove protective backing from the leaves and apply to the candle.
5. Dip the candle twice in the dipping wax.

Candleholder:
A vintage plate

Alphabet and Swirl Sticker Candle

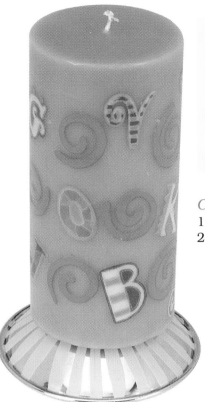

Materials:
- 3" x 6" medium-blue pillar candle
- Colorful alphabet stickers
- Assorted shape stickers (I used orange swirls)
- White dipping wax
- Stainless steel pinch bowl
- Lime-green metal paint

Instructions
1. Apply the swirls and letters over candle.
2. Dip the candle twice in the dipping wax.

Variations:
Use the stickers to spell names or write messages for special occasions.

Candleholder:
1. Paint stripes on the pinch bowl with lime green.
2. Turn the bowl upside down and place candle on top.

Yes Candle

Materials:
- 3" x 4" purple pillar candle
- 'Yes' in alphabet stickers
- One orange beaded scrunchy (hair ornament)
- One lime-green beaded scrunchy
- White dipping wax

Instructions
1. Place the stickers on sides of candle.
2. Dip the candle twice in the dipping wax.
3. Place the scrunchies around the bottom of the candle.

Variations
- Any wording will work using alphabet stickers
- Substitute multi-strand elastic bead bracelets for the scrunchies
- Stretchy napkin rings work as well

Candleholder:
The candle is displayed on a large steamer basket found in the kitchen department.

Canned Food Label Candle

Materials:
- 2 1/2" x 5" pillar candle
- Canned food label trimmed to fit candle
- Silver candle spray paint
- 8 1/2" x 11" sheet double-sided adhesive
- White dipping wax

Instructions
1. Spray candle silver.
2. Cut the double-sided adhesive to fit the label and apply to label.
3. Apply label to candle.
4. Dip the candle twice in the dipping wax.

Candleholder:
Place the candle on a real can as a holder. Any food item will do.

I Love You Stickers Candle

Materials
- Silver 'I Love You' stickers
- 2" x 9" ivory pillar candle
- White dipping wax

Instructions
1. Apply the stickers all over the sides of the candle.
2. Dip the candle twice in the dipping wax.

Candleholder:
Small cut-glass candleholder

Gold Fern on Blue Candle

Materials:

- 3" x 9" dark blue pillar candle
- 8 1/2" x 11" metallic-gold paper
- Emagination Crafts Inc. Punches
  — large grapevine leaf
  — jumbo grapevine leaf
- Tacky glue
- White dipping wax

Instructions

1. Cut a stem for the fern approximately 7" long. Make it approximately 1/4" wide at the bottom and gradually narrowing to a point at the other end. Glue on the candle at an angle.
2. Punch five large leaves and six jumbo leaves from the gold paper.
3. Glue one large leaf at the small end of the stem (the top). Going down the stem, place pairs of leaves exactly opposite each other — 2 large, 2 large, 2 jumbo, 2 jumbo, and 2 jumbo. Leave approximately 1" of stem at the bottom.
4. Dip in twice in the dipping wax.

Candleholder:

Three-footed stand with blue salad plate on top. Space eight jumbo grapevine leaves around the lip of the plate.

Materials

- 3" x 8" ivory candle
- 8 1/2" x 5" metallic-gold paper
- 8 1/2" x 5" sheet of double-sided adhesive
- 4" x 2 1/2" white beaded appliqué bridal accessory
- Tacky glue
- Decorative-edged scissors — wavy
- White dipping wax

Instructions

1. Apply the double-sided adhesive to the back of the gold paper.
2. Cut strips of the gold paper with the wavy edged scissors.
3. Apply the strips to the candle at 1/2" intervals.
4. Dip the candle in the dipping wax twice.
5. Glue the appliqué on the candle.

Sheet Wax

Wax can be bought in very thin sheets that come in a wide variety of colors and make the following candles easy to assemble. Sheet wax has a paper backing, so that you can draw your pattern on the paper and cut it out with scissors or a mat knife. It will stick to itself (layering) or to the candle you are decorating. If the piece is heavy, such as in the Millefiore sample, you may want to put a bit of wax glue between your decoration and the candle.

Fish Bowl Candle

Materials:
- Fish bowl
- Assorted pearls
- 3" x 4" blue candle
- Sheet wax —
  3" x 3"(orange and yellow)
  1/2" x 1/2" (white and black)
- Wax glue by Yaley

Instructions
1. Cut the fish parts out and apply to the candle.
    - Body—orange
    - Fins and tail—yellow
    - Eye—white
    - Center eye—black
2. Cover the bottom of the bowl with pearls.
3. Place candle in the bowl.

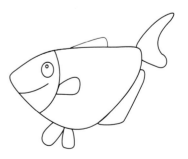

See pattern on page 120.

Millefiore Candle

Materials:

- 1" x 4" strips of sheet wax—assorted colors (three strips per cane) (I made 10 different combination canes to complete my candle.)
- Wax glue by Yaley
- 2.8" white ball candle
- Razor blade or cane cutter (long razor blade)
- Mat knife and mat
- White dipping wax

Instructions

1. Cut three strips, 1" x 4" per cane, of three different colors of sheet wax.
2. Peel off the backing paper and make a tight roll with the first color.
3. At the end of the first color start the second color and then the third and last color.
4. Roll the cane gently in between the palms of your hands.
5. Make several canes of different color combinations.
6. Use the cane cutter to cut slices of the cane approximately 1/8" thick.
7. Apply the cane slices to candle with the wax glue.
8. Dip the candle twice in the dipping wax.

Candleholder:

Black wrought-iron platform candleholder

Christmas Village

Materials

- Candles—
  2" x 2" x 4 1/2"—1 each
  of blue and green
  2" x 2" x 2" - white
  2" x 2" x 6" -yellow
- Sheet wax — black, brown, lavender, dark green, lemon yellow, red, and dark red
- Craft knife and mat
- Ruler
- Wax glue or tacky glue
- Acrylic paint—butter-milk and black
- #0 liner brush
- White dipping wax

Instructions

1. Cut all windows 3/8" x 1" from black wax. Cut all shutters 1/4" x 7/8", all doors 3/4" x 1 3/4", and all windowsills 5/8" x 1/8" from colors that accent your candles.
2. Apply all parts to the houses. Cut trees and apply them to the sides of the end houses if desired.
3. Paint windowpanes with butter-milk acrylic paint using the fine line brush.
4. Add windowsills. Make door knobs by dipping the handle of the paintbrush in paint and applying a dot to the door.
5. Add whipped wax for a snowy winter look or leave plain.

Candleholder:
Beveled wooden plaque painted gray with candles arranged on top

46

Green Tree Sheet Wax Cutout Candle

Materials
- 3" x 6" butterscotch-colored candle
- 5" x 2 1/2" sheet dark green wax
- Wax glue by Yaley
- Tuna can
- 13" leaf ribbons from Loose Ends — forest color

Instructions
1. Cut tree pattern out of sheet wax with scissors or a craft knife.
2. Apply the tree to the candle.

See pattern on page 120.

Candleholder:
Large tuna can turned upside down with 13" length of forest leaf ribbon glued around the outside

Here's a pair of candles that would make a great holiday mantle decoration. Sheet wax gives you the opportunity to make character candles as easily as dressing a doll.

Snowman

Materials:
- 3" x 7 1/2" white Crayon-top candle
- Wax glue or tacky glue
- Sheet wax:
    - 4" x 2"—black (earmuff band, coal eyes and mouth)
    - 2" x 7"—green (earmuff balls and scarf)
    - 2" x 7" – purple (scarf stripes)
    - 2" x 7"—red (scarf)
- One new orange Crayon
- White dipping wax
- Wood-carving tool with large "U" curve
- Decorative-edged scissors—deckle

Instructions
1. Heat wood-carving tool (carving end only) on burner. Twist it in one spot to drill a hole for the crayon nose.
2. Cut out coal shapes for the eyes and mouth and a 1/8" x 4" strip for the earmuffs from the black sheet wax.
3. Cut two 1 1/8" circles from the green sheet wax with the deckle-edged circles. Apply to the candle as earmuff balls.
4. Using the deckle-edged scissors cut out the scarf and stripes for the scarf. Cut two red scarf lengths 7" x 1". Cut four purple strips and two green strips 7" x 1/8". Glue the strips to the scarf piece and fringe one end of each scarf end. Place the scarf around the neck and flip fringed pieces in front of snowman. Spread out the fringe.
5. Dip candle in dipping wax one time.

Santa

Materials

- 9" x 3" red crayon-top candle
- 3" x 3" very heavy card board for feet
- Black acrylic paint
- Wax glue or tacky glue
- Sheet wax:
  - 3 1/2" x 3 1/2" white (beard, mustache, and eyes)
  - 3" x 7" black (belt and boot tops)
  - 3" x 4" red (sleeves)
  - 2 1/2" x 2 1/2" kelly green (mittens)
  - 1" x 1" dark pink (nose) bright pink (cheeks) gold metallic (buckle)
- White whipped wax

Instructions

1. Cut out all the parts. For the belt cut two strips of black 1/2" x 7". Cut two strips of black 3/4" x 7" for the boot tops.
2. Apply all parts to the candle. Let dry. Dip candle one time in the dipping wax.
3. See whipped wax instructions in Chapter 4. Apply whipped wax around the bottom of the hat, around wrists, down center of coat, below the buckle and around the candle to form the bottom of the coat.

See pattern on page 121.

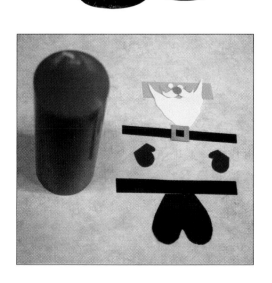

This candle features pre-formed wax decorations in strip form. They come in silver and gold metallic colors. You see this type of trim on the Red Pillar Candle with the Gold Leaves in Chapter 9.

Three Ball Candles with Wax Leaves

Materials:
- Three 2.8" white ball candles
- Finishing Touch Decorative Candle Wax Trims and Accents by Yaley
- Candle dye—yellow, orange, and red
- White dipping wax
- Three sheets of 4" x 8" sheet wax—dark green
- Wax glue by Yaley
- Three tin cans

Instructions
1. Cut the decorative gold strips between the designs. Apply one design to each candle. Evenly space the design on the top half of the candle.
2. Use three separate tin cans, each large enough to accommodate one candle. See dipping wax techniques to determine how much wax will be needed to cover the candle. Place the needed amount of wax into each tin can. Add one dye color to each tin can. Dip a candle four or five times in one color of wax. This will give the candle an intense color but still allow the design to be visible.
3. Cut eight leaves for each candle from the dark green sheet using the leaf. Apply to the bottom half of each candle.

Candleholder:
Displayed on stacked cigar boxes. These candles can be displayed together as a group, or separately as an accent piece.

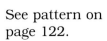

See pattern on page 122.

No-hole beads are another way to add dimension to your candles. No-hole beads are tiny glass marbles that come in sizes from 1.5 mm to the smallest filler beads. Not only do they come in crystal and clear, but in colors like gold, silver, bronze, black crystal, and many more. No-hole beads are attached to the candle with an industrial-strength double-sided adhesive that comes as a tape or a sheet.

Beaded Gold Stars on White Candle

Materials
- 3" x 6" white pillar candle
- Red Liner Star Die Cuts by Craftware
- Gold no-hole 1mm beads
- Gold no-hole filler-size beads

Instructions
1. Apply the adhesive stars to the candle.
2. Remove the protective paper and sprinkle 1mm beads over the stars.
3. Sprinkle the filler beads on stars.

Candleholder:
One large copper star cookie cutter under a 5" round mirror.

Beaded Fruit Candle

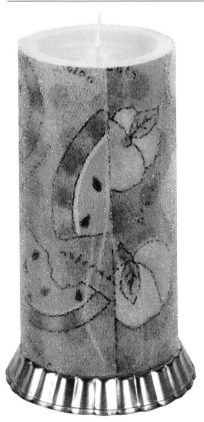

Materials:
- 3" x 6" ivory pillar candle
- 6" x 9" sheet industrial-strength double-sided adhesive
- 1mm crystal glass no-hole beads
- Fruit print tissue paper
- Decoupage medium

Instructions
1. Apply the tissue paper to the candle with the decoupage medium. Let dry completely.
2. Apply the adhesive over the tissue paper.
3. Roll in the no-hole beads until completely covered.

Candleholder:
Displayed on an individual metal gelatin mold turned upside down

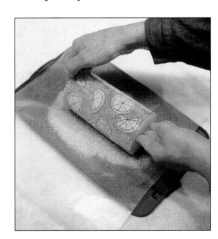

No-hole beads have been combined with bugle beads and seed beads to give the shimmery look on the next two candles.

Bead Flame Candle

Materials
- 3" x 9" crayon-top ivory candle
- 6" x 9" sheet industrial-strength adhesive
- Silver-lined bugle beads
- Clear iridescent seed beads
- Silver filler beads

Instructions
1. Cut the flame design pattern out of adhesive sheet.
2. Apply adhesive to candle. If the pattern doesn't go completely around your candle, copy individual flame patterns to fill in the space.
3. Remove the protective paper from the adhesive.
4. Sprinkle beads in order listed in materials list to cover adhesive.

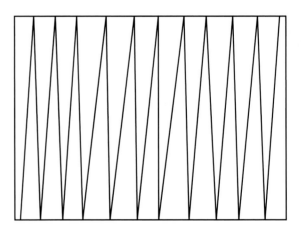

See pattern on page 120.

Candleholder:
3" x 10" wooden post crudely cut and sprayed lightly with ivory paint

Glass Bead Spiral Tapers

Materials:

- 15" ivory taper
- 1/8" x 26" industrial-strength double-sided adhesive tape
- Silver-lined bugle beads
- White iridescent seed beads
- Silver no-hole filler beads

Instructions

1. Start at the top of the taper and spiral the adhesive tape down the taper. Remove the protective paper.
2. Sprinkle beads over the tape in the same order they appear in the material list, ending with the filler beads.

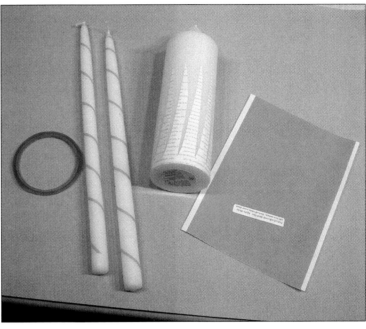

Candleholder:
Glass taper holders can be stacked to vary heights

Fabric Appliqué

Packaged fabric appliqués can be added to candles with double-sided Peel-n-Stick to give an expensive custom-made look.

Purple and Turquoise Mirror Appliqué Candle

Materials
- 3" x 4" dark yellow candle
- Purchased flower and mirror accented appliqués
- Glass and bead adhesive
- Small dowel

Instructions
1. Glue appliqué to candle.

Candleholder:
1. Turn a stainless steel candy dish upside down. Place eight adhesive-backed circles evenly around the base of the dish.
2. Paint the entire dish with lavender metal paint. Remove the stickers. Use turquoise dimensional paint to circle each stainless circle.
3. Use dowel dipped in deep fuchsia to paint dots.

Converted Votive Stand with Beaded Fringe Candle

Materials
- 4" x 4" dark pink pillar candle
- 18" long–wide beaded fringe
- 28 1/2" x 1/4" wide industrial-strength adhesive tape
- Beaded votive stand
- 14" short-beaded fringe
- 3 1/2" circle industrial strength adhesive

Instructions
1. Apply tape to the back of the beaded fringe header.
2. Apply the fringe around the center of the candle so that the beads do not go beyond the bottom of the candle. Save leftover beads for the holder.

Candleholder:
1. I turned a beaded votive stand upside down and removed the seed beads.
2. Apply 1/4" tape to 14" length of short-beaded fringe header.
3. Apply the fringe header to the bottom of the stand platform so that only the fringe hangs down from the platform.
4. Cut a 3 1/2" circle of the adhesive and apply it to the inside of the votive holder platform.
5. Sprinkle the beads left over from the candle fringe to the center of the beaded platform.

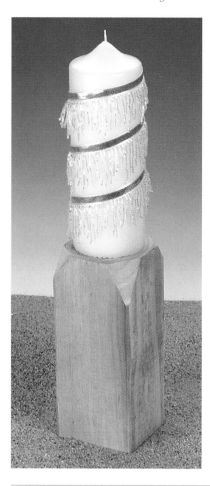

Spiral Bead Fringe Candle

Materials:
- 3" x 8" crayon-top ivory candle
- 28" white iridescent seed bead fringe
- 28" silver metallic 1/8" wide ribbon
- 56" x 1/8" double-sided adhesive tape

Instructions
1. Apply the adhesive to the back of the fringe header. Remove paper from adhesive and apply fringe in a spiral pattern down the candle.
2. Apply adhesive to the back of the silver ribbon. Remove paper from the adhesive and apply the ribbon over the fringe header down the candle.

Candleholder:
3" x 8" post, crudely cut and lightly sprayed with ivory paint

---

Sandpaper Hills Candle

Materials
- 4" x 4" medium green pillar candle
- Four sheets of sandpaper —each a different color brown or black (any size grit will do)
- Tacky glue
- Rubber bands

Candleholder:
I used a black porcelain enamel drip pan from a round gas range burner.

Instructions
1. Cut hill shapes from the sheets of sandpaper. Cut each hill a different height with straight bottoms.
2. Lay the hill on the candle, lining up the bottom edges. Place the hills so that they appear to be different sizes with the tallest closest to the candle.
3. Coat the back of the sandpapers with glue and apply to the candle. Use rubber bands to help hold the hills in place while they dry.
4. Dip the candle three times in dipping wax.

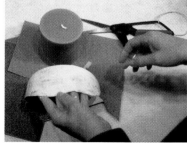

Sandpaper Appliqué with Gold and Copper Candle

Materials:

- 4" x 6" dark red pillar candle
- Two 8 1/2" x 11" sheets coarse (60-grit) sandpaper
- Wavy decorative-edged scissors
- Metallic acrylic paint—gold and copper
- Tacky glue
- Vegetable peeler with a serrated side
- White dipping wax

Instructions

1. Use the decorative-edged scissors to cut the outside edge of the two patterns. Use the regular scissors to cut the inside edge of the pattern. Reverse the pattern for several of the pieces. Cut three large and three small curl patterns.
2. Paint all the pieces on the sand side with the gold paint. Edge all the pieces with the copper. Glue the pieces to the candle.
3. Dip the candle in the dipping wax three times. Let cool completely.
4. Use the serrated edge to grate up and down the candle to form ridges in the overdipped candle.

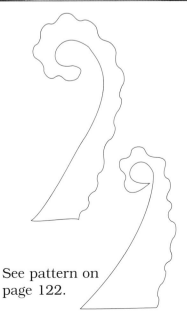

See pattern on page 122.

57

Silver Luggage Tag Monogram Candle

Materials:
- 3" x 8" pillar ivory candle
- Silver alphabet script stickers
- Antique luggage tag ornaments by Supreme Sales
- Gem-Tax Permanent Adhesive

Instructions
1. Place the alphabet initials on the center front about two inches from the top of the candle. Glue the luggage tag frame over the initials.
2. Glue the ornament below the ` tag.

Candleholder:
Decorative wooden disk painted with silver acrylic paint and antiqued by painting with black paint and immediately wiping off the excess. This leaves black paint in the cracks and gives an aged appearance.

Foil and Tattoo Candle

Materials
- 2" x 9" ivory candle
- 11" x 9" heavy-duty aluminum foil
- 9" x 7" sheet double-sided adhesive
- Three Swarovski Tattoos Stars by Creative Crystal
- White dipping wax

Instructions
1. Ball up the aluminum foil. Spread it out and smooth with your hands.
2. Apply the adhesive to the back of the foil.
3. Apply the foil to the candle.
4. Cut jagged pattern out of the adhesive backed foil.
5. Dip the candle twice in the dipping wax.
6. Apply the tattoos on the candle following package instructions.

Candleholder:
Crude wood cut 3" x 3" x 4" and lightly sprayed with ivory paint

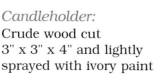

Rhinestone Tattoo Candle

Materials:
- Large white ball candle
- Three Starburst Swarovski Crystal Tattoos by Creative Crystal

Instructions
1. Follow the instructions on the tattoo package. Carefully separate the two foils, making sure that all the stones adhere to the transparent sheet.
2. Apply the stones on the trans parent foil to the candle. Press the foil in place with your hand.
3. Carefully peel off the transparent foil. Place all three tattoos around the candle.

Candleholder:
3" x 3" wooden block cut about 12" tall and sprayed lightly with ivory paint

Candle with Small Mirrors and Rhinestones

Materials:
- 3" x 6" ivory candle
- Mirrors—
    Five 1/2" x 1/2" squares
    Five 3/4" rounds
    Five 1/2" rounds
    Five 1/2" rounds
    Fifteen 2mm rhinestones
- Glass and bead adhesive

Instructions
1. Five rows of round mirrors should be evenly spread around the candle. Bottom mirror is: 3/4" round, topped by 1/2" round, 1/4" round, and three 2mm rhinestones.
2. Squares go in between. Position the squares with one corner of mirror pointed down.

Candleholder:
3" x 3" wooden block cut 6" tall and sprayed lightly with ivory paint

Button Candle

Materials
- Assorted colors and sizes of buttons
- Green 3" x 6" pillar candle
- Glass and bead adhesive

Instructions
1. Lay the candle on its side.
2. Glue the buttons onto the candle. Do one side and let the glue dry completely before you turn the candle.
3. Turn the candle and add buttons as desired until the candle sides are covered.

Candleholder:
Painted ceramic teapot with the lid on upside down to support the candle.

Candles with Nature's Add-ons: Real, Preserved and Just a few Artificial

Real Bark Candle

Materials:
- 3" x 4" butterscotch candle
- Real bark from a river birch tree (I got mine from my neighbor's tree, but you can purchase bark from Loose Ends)
- Tacky glue
- Waxed paper
- Rubber band

Instructions
Note: River birch trees shed their bark in sheets. The sheet of bark is as thin as a sheet of paper.

1. Paint glue on the back side of the bark. Apply to candle. Apply as many sheets as needed to cover the sides of the candle. Overlap the bark as needed.
2. To keep the bark around the candle while the glue is drying, roll waxed paper tightly around the bark-covered candle and secure with several rubber bands. When the glue is dry remove the rubber bands and waxed paper.

Horsetail Reed Candle

Materials:
- Horsetail Reed by Loose Ends
- Tacky glue
- 4" x 4" brown pillar candle
- White dipping wax

Instructions
1. Cut pieces to height of candle or to desired height. Do not go taller than the candle. On a tall candle, you could cut the reeds to cover only a section at the bottom. Glue pieces of the reed to the sides of the candle.
2. Overdip the entire candle in white dipping wax.

Shell Candle on Metal Thimble

Materials

- 4" x 4" ivory pillar candle
- Assorted shells
- Glass and bead adhesive
- Assorted small shells
- Opalescent flat marbles
- White dipping wax
- Adjustable aluminum wall thimble (from hardware store)
- Tacky glue

Instructions

1. Glue the shells around the bottom of the candle. Let dry completely.
2. Dip the candle in the dipping wax twice.

Candleholder

1. Alternate shells with the marbles and glue them on top of the thimble.
2. Place the candle on top.

Galax Leaves and Frog

Materials

- 3" x 9" medium green pillar candle
- Four preserved galax leaves with stems from Loose Ends
- 3 yards thin gold cord
- Kaolin frogs from Wang's International
- Tacky glue

Instructions

1. Use the tacky glue to attach the leaves to the candle.
2. Wrap the gold cord around the stem end of the leaf about two-thirds up the length of the candle from the bottom. Tie the ends in a knot and clip the excess. Leave a tail approximately 1 1/2" long.
3. Glue the frog on the front of the candle in the top upper portion.

Candleholder:
4" round mirror

Bug and Ivy

Materials:
- 3" x 6" moss green pillar candle
- 2" brass bug charm from Creative Beginnings
- Two large ivy leaves with wire stems
- Tacky glue
- Needle-nose pliers

Instructions
1. Dip the ends of the leaf wires in glue to keep them from raveling. Use the needle-nose pliers to curl the wire into a coil.
2. Glue the leaves on the candle after interlocking the wire coils.
3. Glue the bug above the leaves.

Candleholder:
Upside-down brass planter

Red Candles with Gold Painted Leaves

Materials:
- 4" x 6" red pillar candle
- 2" x 9" red pillar candle
- Eight plain gold stripes Finishing Touch Decorative Candle Wax Trims and Accents by Yaley
- Silk leaves that have been painted gold
- Heavy mat board
- Tacky glue

Instructions:
1. Decorate the 9" candle by applying the gold wax stripes vertically around the candle.
2. Add leaves to the bottom portion of the large candle.

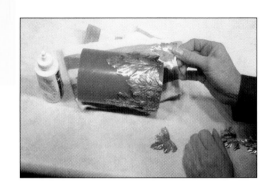

Candleholder:
1. Cut two mat board circles 1/2" larger than each candle. Glue six small leaves around the small circle and seven large leaves around the large candle.
2. When completely dry, place the candles on the leaf circles.

Gold Metallic Frog and Braid Candle

Materials:
- 3" x 6" dark green candle
- Gold metallic-trim frog closure by Wrights
- 7 feet of gold middy braid by Wrights
- Tacky glue

Instructions

1. Wrap the braid around the center of the candle. Bury the first end as you go and glue the braid as you go. Tack the last end of the braid under the wrap.
2. Glue the frog on the front of the braid wrap.

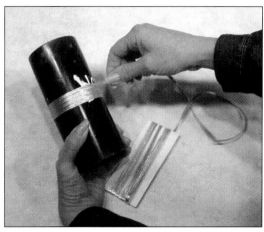

Candleholder:
4" round mirror

Copper Mesh with Gold Star Ornament

Materials
- 3" x 7" white crayon-top candle
- 18" copper mesh knitted tube by Loose Ends
- 45" copper 20-gauge wire
- Purchased gold wire star ornament

Instructions
1. Roll up bottom and roll down top of copper mesh tube.
2. Place tube over candle
3. Wrap the wire around the candle as many times as it will reach. Add star ornament to wire. Twist ends together and cut off excess wire.

Candleholder:
Brass-footed pillar candleholder

Sea Glass Candle

Materials:
- 3" x 6" medium green pillar candle
- Sea glass—blues, greens and clear
- Dipping wax
- Glass and bead adhesive

Instructions
1. Lay the candle on its side on top of a dishcloth. This will keep it from rolling.
2. Glue the sea glass all over the candle. Do one section at a time and let that section dry completely before turning the container. Let entire candle dry completely before going to the next step.
3. Dip the candle in dipping wax four times.

Candleholder:
Display on a wire-beaded basket candleholder decorated with wire and marbles (see the candleholder section for instructions).

Wrapping a candle with wire is a stress-free way to add an unusual touch to your decorating. The next two candles illustrate this style.

Brown Wire and River Rock on Butterscotch Candle

Materials
- 4" x 6" butterscotch-colored candle
- Wire—
  60" brown 10-gauge
  60" copper 16-gauge
- Large, black river rock
- Needle-nose pliers

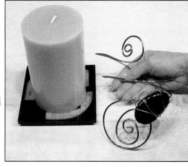

Instructions
1. Use the needle-nose pliers to coil ends of the wire. The top coil is small and loose and about 2" in diameter.
2. The bottom coil is a large loose coil with about a 3 1/2" diameter.
3. The middle section is wrapped around the candle twice with coils on the front side of the candle.
4. Wrap the river rock with 16-gauge wire and wire the rock to the 10-gauge wire above the large bottom coil.
5. Place the wire over the candle.

Candleholder:
Square picture frame with the back removed and four black wooden disks as feet

Copper Wire Wrap on Burgundy Candle

Materials:
- 2" x 9" burgundy pillar candle
- 72" copper 10-gauge wire
- Needle-nose pliers

Instructions
1. Using the needle-nose pliers, coil the beginning and the end of the wire.
2. Wrap the coil around the candle with coil endings in front.

Note: Use the candle as a guide for size, but substitute a paper towel roll to wrap the wire around so you don't scar the candle while twisting the wire. If the coil is made wider than the candle it can be slipped off and used on another candle.

Candleholder:
Wooden disk painted gold

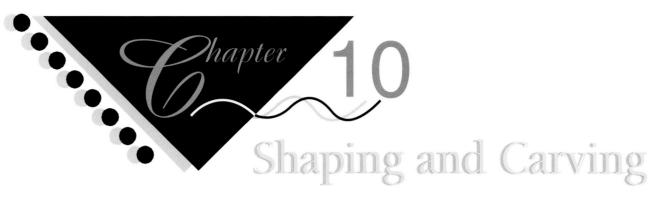

Chapter 10

Shaping and Carving

You can change the shape of a candle by adding to or removing from its surface. The following group of candles includes techniques on carving, scratching, and whipping. We'll make those candles behave!

Candles with Whipped Wax, Shells and Pearls

Materials:
- 4" x 7" white triangular candle
- 4" x 4" square candle
- Assorted shells
- Assorted pearl beads
- White whipped wax (See Chapter 4)
- Fork

Instructions
1. Whip the wax and use the fork to apply it to the candles. As you apply the wax add shells and pearls. Gently press them into the candles.
2. Continue until the candles are covered. Do not cover the wick.
3. Let the candles cool completely before picking them up.

Candleholder
Use a metal charger or dessert plate.

Gold and Silver Metallic Scratched Tapers

Materials:

- 12" gold metallic taper
- 12" silver metallic taper
- Acrylic paint—black
- Candle painting medium
- Scratching tool (sewing needle or sharp stylus)
- Rag

Instructions

1. Use the scratching tool to scratch designs all over the tapers.
2. Mix one part black paint and one part candle medium. Paint mixture all over tapers.
3. Immediately remove the paint with the rag. The paint will remain in the scratches.

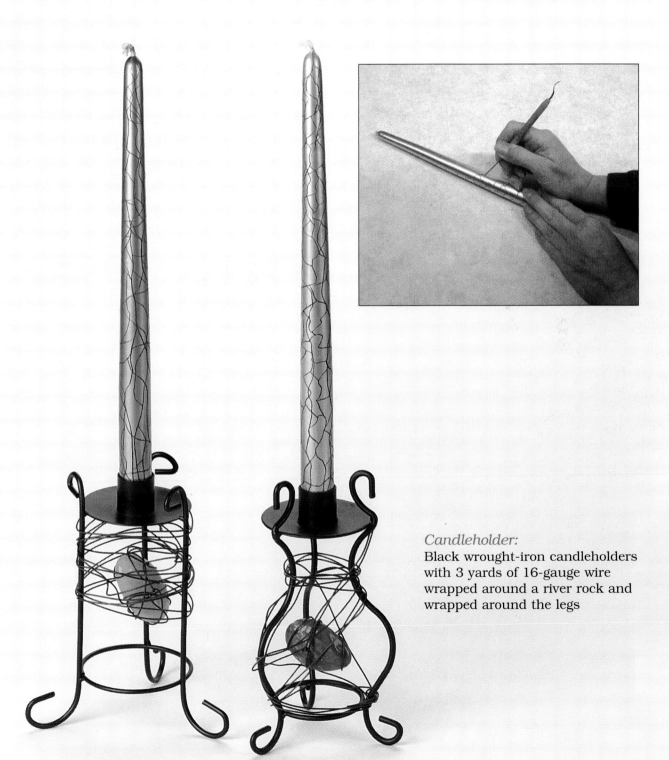

Candleholder:

Black wrought-iron candleholders with 3 yards of 16-gauge wire wrapped around a river rock and wrapped around the legs

Green Metallic Taper with Copper Paint

Materials
- 12" green metallic taper
- Small 'V' wood-carving tool
- Acrylic paint—copper
- #1 liner brush
- Candle painting medium

Instructions
1. Use V tool to carve out approximately 3/4"-long gouges along the candle.
2. Mix the copper paint with an equal amount of candle medium. Paint the inside of the gouges with copper paint mixture.

Cracked Look Candles

Materials:
- Ivory and dark green pillar candles (any size will work)
- Scratching tool, such as large upholstery needle
- Acrylic paint—buttermilk and raw umber
- Faux glazing medium
- Paintbrush
- Paper towels or rags

Instructions
1. Using the scratching tool, make lines in the candle surface. Vary the width of the mark by varying how hard you press the your tool and by how much wax you remove with each scratch.
2. Mix one part paint to one part glazing medium. Brush on the candle. Use the buttermilk on the green candle and the raw umber on the ivory candles. Immediately wipe off the excess paint with the paper towel. The paint will be left in the cracks.

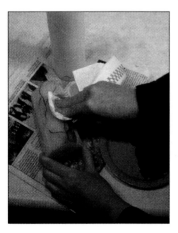

Tapers Textured with Kitchen Utensil

Materials

- Two 12" tapers (blue and butterscotch)
- Serrated-edged kitchen tool (any object with sharp serrated edge)
- Viridian green acrylic paint
- Rags

Instructions

1. Use the serrated edge on the blue taper by pulling the edge from top to bottom in an uneven pattern.
2. Use the serrated edge on the butterscotch taper by making a crosshatched pattern with an up and down strokes.
3. Coat both tapers with green paint and immediately wipe off the excess with a rag.

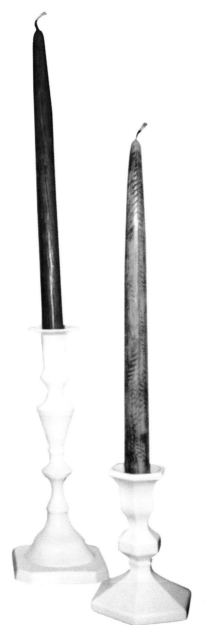

Candleholder:
Old brass candleholder painted with ivory paint

Gold Leaf Log

Materials

- 2" x 9" dark green pillar candle with a flat top
- V-shaped wood-carving tool for gouging
- Gold leaf kit from Houston Art Inc. (includes gold leaf, sizing, and sealer)
- Soft paintbrush
- Variegated Black Metal Leaf from Houston Art Inc.

Instructions

1. Carve wood-grain look into candle with V-shaped tool.
2. Paint sizing onto uncarved sections of candle. (See packaging for instructions on using gold leaf kit).
3. Apply gold leaf to the candle. Use soft paintbrush to remove excess.
4. Paint sealer on candle.

Chapter 11

Color Variation

White dipping wax can be colored for dipping pre-made candles to change or add to their original color. If you have a color theme, you can custom make your special color by combining several dye colors together (see dying in the technique section). There are infinite possibilities when dipping for color. I have a few candles in this section to help you get started.

String-Wrapped Pillar Candle Dipped in Coral Wax

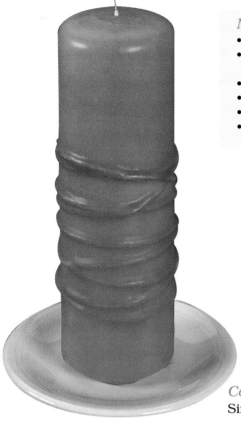

Materials:
- 3" x 9" white pillar candle
- Cotton cord (approximately 3 yards)
- Plastic sandwich bag
- Tacky glue
- Coral candle dye
- White dipping wax

Instructions
1. Squirt several tablespoons of tacky glue into the sandwich bag. Place the cotton cord in the bag. Seal the bag and squish the glue into the cord.
2. Pull the string out of the bag and wrap it around the center portion of the candle. Let it dry.
3. Mix the candle dye in the white wax (see Chapter 4).
4. Dip the candle seven times in the coral wax.

Candleholder:
Simple ivory saucer

String-Wrapped Tapers with Gradual Coral Dye Dip

Materials:
- Two 12" white taper candles
- One-yard cotton cord per candle
- Tacky glue
- Plastic sandwich bag
- Coral candle dye
- White dipping wax

Candleholder:
Frosted 2 1/2" taper holder

Instructions:
1. Follow instruction steps 1 through 3 for String-Wrapped Pillar Candle.
2. To achieve a gradual color change dip whole tapers one time. Keep dipping the candle and each time dip less of the length of the candle. The results will be a darker coral color at the bottom with the candle getting lighter towards the top.

Note: These candles were too tall for my dipping vat. They were dipped first from the top and then from the bottom to cover them completely the first dip.

Following are several colored candles that illustrate the gradation dipping technique. This technique colors a candle gradually from light to dark. Light-colored candles pop dramatically with this technique and dark-colored candles show a more subtle color change.

Graduated Blue Dye and Butterscotch Candle

Materials:
- 4" x 4" butterscotch candle
- Turquoise candle dye
- 6" storm collar (from the hardware store)
- 3" storm collar
- Butterscotch-colored river rocks

Instructions:
1. Dissolve the turquoise dye in white wax.
2. Make graduated dips (see Chapter 4). Make the first dip within 1" of the top of the candle. Each time you dip the candle, dip a little less of the candle so that the darkest and most dipped portion is the bottom.

Candleholder:
1. Place the 6" storm collar large side up.
2. Place the 3" storm collar inside the first with the largest side down. Place the candle on top.
3. Arrange butterscotch-colored river rocks in the indention formed by the two collars in a circle around the candle.

Denture-Cleanser Overdip with Wire and Bead Trim

Materials:
- 3" x 6" light blue pillar candle
- 8 1/2" x 11" purple handmade paper
- Decoupage medium
- 24 effervescent denture cleanser tablets
- White dipping wax
- 3 yards silver 28-gauge wire
- Assorted small bead in greens and blues

Instructions
1. Tear the purple paper into irregular strips. Apply strips around the candle with decoupage medium. Let dry completely.
2. Dip candle twice in dipping wax. Let cool.
3. See displacement rules in Chapter 4. Fill a second container with water. Drop in denture tablets. Lower candle in container, then immediately dip candle into dipping wax.

Candleholder:
1. Place beads on wire at 3" intervals and twist wire to hold in place.
2. Place the candle on an upside-down purple soup bowl and loosely wrap beaded wire into a circle around the base of the candle.

Blue Gradated Candle Overdipped in Dental Cleanser

Materials:
- 3" x 8" dark blue candle
- Coral dye
- White dipping wax
- 24 effervescent denture cleanser tablets
- 3 yards silver 28-gauge wire
- Assorted small bead in greens and blues

Instructions:
1. Dissolve the coral dye in the white dipping wax.
2. Make graduated dips starting at the middle of the candle. Each time you dip the candle, dip a little less of the candle so that the darkest and most dipped portion is the bottom. Let cool.
3. See displacement rules in Chapter 4. Fill a second container with water. Drop in denture tablets. Lower candle into container, then immediately dip candle into dipping wax.

Candleholder:
1. Place beads on wire at 3" intervals and twist wire to hold in place.
2. Place the candle on an upside-down white saucer and loosely wrap beaded wire into a circle around the base of the candle.

Color-Drip Candles

Materials:
- Two white crayon-top candles
- Four tin cans
- Candle dye (red, yellow, orange, and blue)
- White dipping wax
- Two white pillar candles
- Drinking straws
- Toothpick or pointed end of wooden skewer
- Cone-shaped stem glass
- Beaded fringe
- Tacky glue
- crayons (24 pack)
- Mat board

Instructions
1. Put one color of dye in each tin can and add hot wax. Put all four cans in double boiler (see dye technique).
2. Use the straw in the lightest-color (yellow) wax first. Place the straw in the wax and put your finger over the top of the straw to trap wax inside the straw. Hold the straw over the candle and wiggle your finger so that wax drops out of the straw onto the candle.
3. After you have done this several times with the yellow wax move on to the orange and repeat procedure.
4. Repeat using red wax and finish with blue wax.
5. To make the dots on the candle, dip the pointed end of the skewer or the toothpick into the hot wax. Remove from wax and, after the excess has run off the tip, touch it to the candle to make a raised dot of wax. Repeat the color order to make the dots.

Candleholder:
1. Cone-shaped stem glass turned upside down.
2. Glue beaded fringe around the bottom of glass above the stem.

Variation
Lay the candle on its side and use above technique

Candleholder:
1. Cut mat board into 3" x 3" square.
2. Layer and glue crayons (see photo above).
3. Place candle on top of crayons.

Multicolored Dipped Taper

Materials:
- Butterscotch-colored taper
- Orange- and red-dyed wax
- Triangular piece of wood painted black
- 3/4" PVC pipe fitting
- 45" of 18-gauge copper wire

Instructions:
1. Dip the top 1/3 of the taper in the orange wax several times. Let cool.
2. Dip the bottom 1/3 of candle in red wax several times. Let cool.

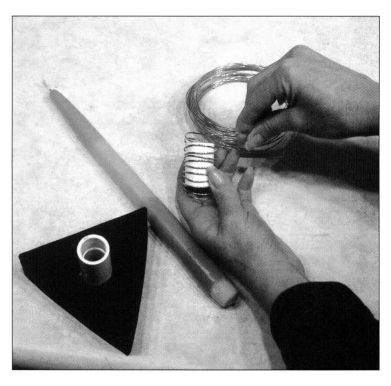

Candleholder:
1. Paint a triangular piece of wood black.
2. Glue a 3/4" PVC pipefitting to the center of the triangle.
3. Wrap the 45" of copper wire loosely around candle.

Variation:
Make a half-twist white taper and dip the top half of the candle in red wax and the bottom half in orange wax.

Texture can be added to a candle with hot wax. Here are several ways to apply the wax and texture.

Spice Rolls

Looking for a texture lift for your candles? Don't forget to check your spice rack. Spices and herbs aren't just for adding scent to your candles but can also be a feast for the eyes.

Crushed Red Pepper Candle

Materials:
- 3" x 6" butterscotch-colored pillar candle
- Crushed red peppers (not pepper flakes)
- White dipping wax
- Cookie sheet or large pan lined with aluminum foil
- Two individual metal gelatin molds
- Screw and nut

Instructions
1. Pour crushed peppers into lined pan.
2. Dip candle in dipping wax seven times.
3. Immediately roll candle in crushed peppers.
4. With hands, press peppers into wax or you can roll the candle on a hard, clean surface.
5. Dip the candle into the dipping wax.

Candleholder:
1. Place two metal gelatin molds with bottoms together.
2. Use screw and nut to fasten them together.
3. Place the candle on top.

Mustard Seed and Assorted Pepper Candle

Materials:

- 3" x 6" red pillar candle
- Mustard seeds
- Assorted peppercorns
- White dipping wax
- Two cooking sheets lined with the aluminum foil
- Miniature galvanized tub

Instructions:

1. Pour mustard seeds into the foil-lined cookie sheet.
2. Dip only the bottom half of the candle seven times.
3. Immediately roll the candle in mustard seeds.
4. Let the candle cool completely.
5. Pour assorted peppercorns into the second cookie sheet.
6. Hold the candle upside down and dip the top half of the candle only seven times.
7. Immediately roll the candle in the peppercorns.
8. Dip the entire candle one time in the dipping wax.

Candleholder:

Upside-down miniature galvanized tub

Candle Log with Brown Bark

Materials:

- 3" x 6" green pillar candle with flat top
- White dipping wax
- Brown wax dye
- 3/4" x 2" sponge

Instructions

1. Add brown dye to small amount of dipping wax. Remove the wax from the heat and let cool to 160°.
2. Dip the sponge in the brown wax and draw the sponge down the candle. Repeat all over the candle sides. Make strokes down the candle length. Use long strokes to cover and shorter strokes to represent bark segments.

Chapter 13
Stacking and Wrapping

S tack small candles on one wick to form a new candle. Do not use votives or tea lights for this because they are made of wax that liquefies when hot.

Flower Pot Candles

Materials:
- Purchased flower floating candle
- 3" x 3" pillar candles with flat top
- Candle wick approximately 8" long
- Wick-holder tab
- Wicking needle
- Ice pick
- Needle-nose pliers
- Wax glue by Yaley

Instructions

1. To remove the wicks in the pillar and floating candle, first remove the wick-holder tab on the bottom of the candles. Try to pull the wick out of the candle with the pliers. If this doesn't work, heat the end of the ice pick and gently push it into the wick hole from the bottom and from the top of the candle until the wick pulls out.
2. Prepare the new wick and attach the wick-holder tab. Push the wick up from the bottom of the pillar candle. Smear wax glue on the bottom of the flower candle and thread the flower candle onto the wick. Trim the wick.
3. Dip the candle once or twice in the dipping wax.

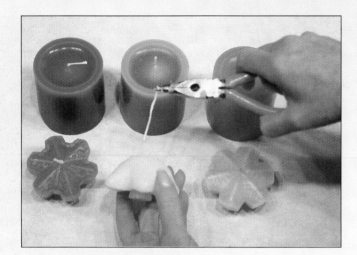 

Candleholder:
Terra cotta pot saucers slightly larger than the candles.

Materials:

- Slab of white wax (it comes from the store like this)
- Hammer
- Metal skewer
- Prepared wick
- Wicking needle

Instructions:

1. Place the wax on a clean sheet of paper over a hard surface. Place a second sheet of paper on top of the wax.
2. Hit the sheet of wax with the hammer and break it into iceberg-like pieces.
3. Heat the end of the skewer on the burner. Lay the iceberg piece of wax on its side and slowly push the skewer into the candle from the center bottom. Let the hot skewer do the work. Don't force the skewer through or the wax will break. Continue the process of heating the tip of the skewer and gently push until the end of the skewer comes out of the top of the candle.
4. Thread the wick up through the candle and add the candlewick tab at the bottom of the wick. Trim the wick.

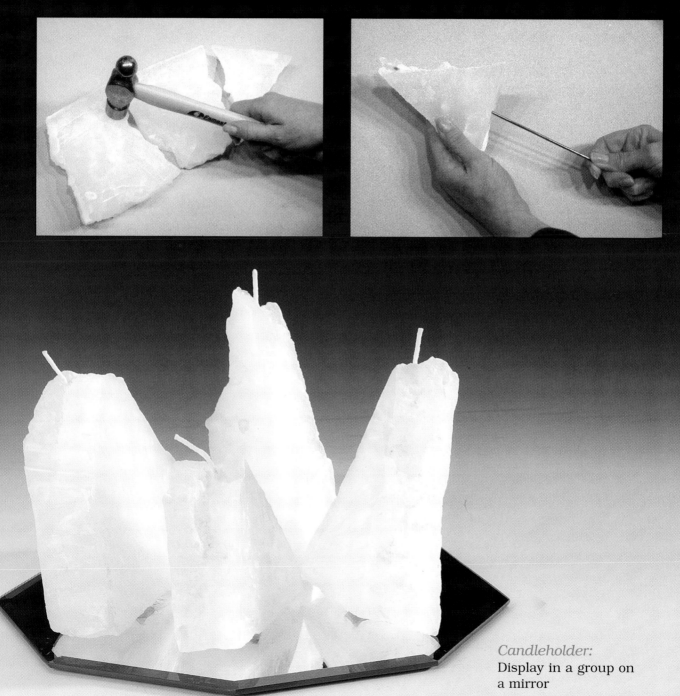

Candleholder:
Display in a group on a mirror

Candleholder:
I used a white chip-and-dip bowl. I placed the candle where the dip goes and black river rocks where the chips go.

Stacked Square Candle

Materials:

- 7 or more 5" x 5" square plastic sandwich keepers
- 12" wick
- Ice pick
- White dipping wax
- Metal skewer
- Wick-holder tabs
- 4" wooden dowel

Instructions

1. Mark all plastic containers at a 1/2" level.
2. Pour wax in containers and let cool.
3. When the wax is set, turn the containers upside down and pull out on sides of containers until the wax sides become free. Set the container on a flat surface, upside down, and press down on the container until the wax pops free.
4. You will need to poke a hole in the center of each square with a hot skewer.
5. Prepare the wick and make it extra long.
6. Stack the squares, staggering the corners.
7. Insert the wick into the candle. At the bottom of the candle, pull 5" of wick onto the wick-holder tab. Use the pliers to bend and push the tab into the bottom of the candle. Tie remainder of the wick around the dowel and dip into the dipping wax holding the top of the wick with pliers. Dip several times.
8. Remove the dowel at the bottom and trim the wick under the tab. Trim the wick at the top of the candle.

Note: I used the dowel for dipping because the candle is too heavy for the wick holder tab.

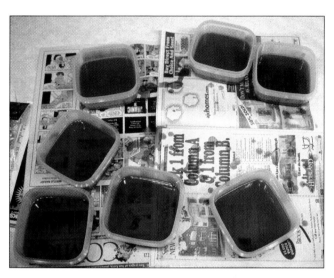

Coffee Cup and Saucer Candle

Materials:

- Cup and saucer
- Votive candle that is correct height for level of "coffee"
- Brown candle dye
- White dipping wax
- Tin can

Instructions:

1. Place the votive in the cup.
2. Melt paraffin in tin can. Use approximately one cup of wax. Add enough dye to obtain coffee color.
3. Pour the wax over the votive candle in the cup until the level is even with the votive. Do not cover the wick.
4. After the wax has set, fill in any indentations in top of the candle with more brown wax.
5. Place the cup on the saucer.

Candle and Shells in a Mold

Materials:

- 3 1/2" x 4 1/2" square embedding Buddy Mold by Yaley
- Mold Sealer by Yaley
- 2" x 4 1/2" white candle
- Assorted shells
- White dipping wax

Instructions

1. Use the mold sealer on the outside bottom of the mold to seal the wick holder.
2. Center the candle inside the mold and fill in the outer area with shells (try to position them so the pretty side is facing outward).
3. Pour hot wax, 180° to 190°, into the mold. Let candle sit. Fill in any indentations that form as the wax hardens.
4. When the wax cools, release the candle from the mold. If the candle does not come out easily, place the molded candle in the refrigerator for an hour. This will make it easier to remove.
5. If you would like more of the shells to show, use a heat gun to melt some of the outer wax.

Candleholder:
I used a small aluminum tray filled with lentils and placed the candle on top.

Pour-and-Roll Red Candle

Materials:

- Leftover hot wax
- Additives (if desired—spices, potpourri, etc.)
- Large, 2"-deep cookie sheet or broiler pan
- Aluminum foil
- Prepared wick approximately 14" long
- Knife

Instructions:

1. Line the cookie sheet with foil.
2. Spread the additives over the foil.
3. Pour the hot wax over the foil 1/8" to 1/2" thick.
4. While the wax is warm, remove the foil.
5. Cut off the edges and cut wax at an angle. For example, cut the tallest end 7" to the shortest end at 5".
6. Lay the wick on the tall end and roll the candle. Stand the candle up to cool.
7. Trim wick.

Chapter 14
Presentation

Sometimes it's the holder and not the candle that becomes the star!

Storm Candles

Yes, you've seen them before they are called storm candles. They are inexpensive candles usually set aside for power outages. When lit, they have a beautiful glow and are quite stunning luminaries. Following are a few ways to use them.

Three Storm Candles Covered with Handmade Shadow Paper

Materials:
- Mindoro "Shadow" Paper by Loose Ends—14" x 8" strip each: Twigs, ferns, and bamboo
- Three 14" x 8" double-sided adhesive sheets
- Three storm candles

Instructions
1. Apply the adhesive sheets to the back of each Mindoro paper.
2. Apply paper to the glass.

Variation
1. Wrap 18" length of copper wire around the top of the glass and use a pliers to twist the wire three or four times to tighten it around the candle glass.
2. Trim the ends to the wire about 1/2" below the twist.

Candleholder:
Displayed on a long, narrow mirror in a silver frame. Each candle sits in a glass ashtray filled with black beans.

Black-and-Gold Tassel Cord Storm Candle Cover

Materials:

- Storm candle
- 14" x 8" and 20" x 6" gold crinkle tissue paper
- Black and gold tassels with cord
- Rubber band

Instructions:

1. Wrap 14" x 8" piece of tissue around the storm candle and glue ends together. Do not glue the paper to the glass so that it can be removed and put on a new candle when this one burns down.
2. Fold top and bottom of the 20" x 6" piece of tissue in to form a 20" x 3" strip. Glue ends together.
3. Put a rubber band around the candle 2" down from the top of the glass. Put 20" x 3" strip under the rubber band and evenly distribute around the candle.
4. Double wrap the tassel cord around the candle and tie in a double knot in front of the candle.
5. Reach inside the tassel and push the tassel up the cords. Tie a new knot under the tassel and cut off the excess cord.

Gold Tassel and Washi Paper

Materials:

- Storm Candle
- Japanese Washi Paper from Aitoh Company
  —14" x 8" sheet with beiges, green, cream, and blue fan print
  —2 1/4" x 14" with peach floral print
- Gold tassels with gold cord

Instructions

1. Wrap the 14" x 8" paper around the storm candle and glue at the back seams.
2. Fold the peach paper 1/2" in along the top and the bottom. Wrap around the glass 1 1/2" down from the top of the glass.
3. Wrap the gold cord around the glass over the peach paper. Wrap twice and tie a double knot in the cord.
4. Reach inside the tassel and push tassel up the cords. Tie a new knot under the tassel and cut off the excess cord.

Glass Vase with Fringe and Flames of Beads

Materials:

- Glass vase 14" wide at the top and 4" tall
- 15" white iridescent bead fringe
- 15" silver metallic ribbon (1/8" wide)
- Two sheets 6" x 9" industrial-strength double-sided adhesive
- Silver-lined glass bugle beads
- No-hole glass beads
  —pearl 1.5mm
  —silver 1mm
  —silver filler
- Glass and bead adhesive
- Glass storm candle
- 12 mirrors—six 3/4" rounds and six 1/2" rounds
- Paper and pencil to draw up flame pattern

Instructions:

1. Glue the header of the fringe around the top edge of the vase.
2. Glue the silver ribbon over the fringe header.
3. Draw out your own flame pattern, varying the bottoms of the flames from 3/4" wide to 1/2" wide.
5. Apply the flames to the bottom of the vase. Remove the protective paper.
6. Sprinkle the beads on the adhesive in the order they are appear on the materials list, ending with the silver-filler beads.
7. Glue the mirrors randomly on glass storm candle.
8. Place the storm candle inside the vase.

Glass Votive Holder with Beaded Glass Lip

Materials:
- 2" x 3" glass votive holder
- White votive candle
- 1/2" x 7" industrial-strength adhesive tape
- Beads
  —silver-line bugle beads
  —iridescent white seed beads
  —silver glass no-hole filler beads

Instructions
1. Apply the adhesive to the lip of the votive holder.
2. Remove the protective paper from the adhesive and sprinkle with the beads in the same order as they appear on the materials list. Finish with the silver no-hole beads.

Candleholder:
4" round mirror.

Crystal Chandelier

Materials:
- Old chandelier light fixture
- 30 yards of 24-gauged silver wire
- Eight 32 x 9mm acrylic crystal pendants
- Large assortment of sizes and shapes of crystal beads
- Five crystal taper holders
- Five ivory, 5" molded tapers
- Ivory spray paint

(All acrylic crystal beads from The Beadery)

Instructions:

1. Remove all electric wires and light bulb housing from the chandelier. Clean chandelier and let it dry completely.
2. Spray paint chandelier with ivory paint.
3. Assemble five drops on each arm of the chandelier as follows: Cut the silver wire 12". Thread the pendant to 1" from the end of the wire. Fold the 1" tail back up to the wire and twist to secure the pendant. Be sure that the first several beads cover the twist.

   The next beads are as follows:
   - 6mm round
   - 11mm heart
   - 6mm round
   - 14mm round
   - 24 x 11mm elongated bicone
   - 12mm disc
   - 13 x 6mm-elongated bicone
   - 10 6mm rounds

   Wrap the 10 top beads around one of the arms of the chandelier. Thread the end of the wire back through the 10 6mm rounds and cut off the end.

4. This configuration covers the center bottom of the chandelier. Start with two 36" lengths of wire. Thread both wires through a large crystal pendant and center it on the wires. Run all of the wires though a 12 mm disc. Separate all four wires and add the following beads to each:
   - 6mm round
   - 24 x 11 elongated bicone
   - 6mm round
   - 13 x 6mm elongated bicone
   - 6mm round

   Thread onto one of the four wires:
   - 18mm round
   - 18 x 16mm squatty bicone

   Pick up the next wire and, holding the two wires together, add the same two-bead pattern to both wires. Pick up the third wire and, holding the three wires together, add the same bead pattern. Pick up the fourth wire and add the last two-bead pattern. This makes eight bead groups in a horizontal circle.

   Push wires through the circle and bring one end out every two beads. Add 20 6mm rounds to each wire. Make the last horizontal circle by threading the five 8mm rounds onto one wire, pick up the second wire and add five more to both wires. Pick up the third wire and add five more beads to the three wires and pick up the fourth wire and complete the pattern. Place the circle of 8mm beads around the top of the chandelier center bottom section and twist the wires together with the pliers to secure the circle to the chandelier. Trim the excess wire and bury the ends by pushing into beads.

5. Thread the beads on to a wire approximately 7 1/2 to 8 yards long. Alternate small with large beads for contrast. Start and end wire with a pendant bead. Use this string of beads to drape around the chandelier twice. Secure the last pendant around the center of the chandelier. Add the crystal candleholders and candles. Hang securely.

Kitchen utensils can become eye-catching sconces with a touch of wire and beads.

Skimmer Sconces

Materials:

- 1 sconce
- Wire
  —45" of 10-gauge base copper wire
  —36" of 16-gauge tinned copper
  —36" of 20-gauge tinned copper
- 13 10mm silver-tone jump rings
- Glass beads
  —47 silver-lined rochaille E beads
  —Seven red-barrel beads 19 x 6mm
  —Seven orange small barrel beads
    9 x 6mm
  —Seven yellow-faceted 7mm
  —Seven turquoise round 9mm
  —Seven purple disc 9mm
  —12 green disc 9mm
  —13 green seed beads
- Red glass cabochon
- 13 brass-head pins (2" nickel-plated)
- Candle or votive holder and candle
- Needle-nose pliers
- Glass and bead adhesive

Instructions

1. Bend bottom of skimmer so that it can sit flat on your work surface.
2. Add one green seed bead to all head pins. On six of the pins add these beads: red barrel, green disc, orange barrel, and four E beads. On the seven remaining pins add the turquoise round, yellow faceted, purple disc and six E beads. Make a loop at the top of each pin and attach them to the jump rings. Alternate beads starting with the turquoise, yellow, purple, combination. Alternate colors and attach them to the outer ring of holes in the skimmer. Skip one hole between.
3. Use the needle-nose pliers to curl both ends of the 10-gauge bare copper wire. Place one loop over hole at the top of the skimmer handle. Wrap around the handle twice and make a cursive 'J' shape on the left side of the handle with the end of the wire coil over the handle.
4. With one end of the 16-gauge wire, come through the hole in the handle from the back and wrap around the copper coil once. Bring the remainder of the 16-gauge wire around the front of the handle over the copper wrap and wrap around the handle twice. Wrap the wire around the 10-gauge wire all along the 'J' design. Add 9mm disc beads every few wraps. Hide the end.
5. Make a small loop in one end of the 20-gauge tinned copper wire and add turquoise round bead, red barrel bead, green disc, and six E beads.
6. Wrap the wire above the E beads around red cabochon several times. Add glue to the back of the cabochon. Let dry. Attach to wire design at the center of the 'J'.
7. Add candle.

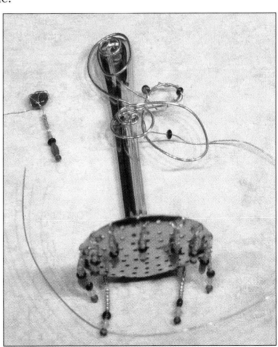

Candle lamps are a great way to add light and a wonderful canvas for shade covers. The covers can be changed as often as the tea lights inside.

Copper Star Cookie Cutter Votive Shield

Materials:
- Large copper star shaped cookie cutter
- 6" gold doilies
- 6" x 6" gold iridescent vellum
- Glass votive holder
- Red votive candle
- Tacky glue

Instructions:
1. When you remove doilies from the package they stick together. Keep three doilies intact and punch out any of the cutouts that haven't been removed. Glue the doily to the gold vellum. Let dry completely.
2. Place the cookie cutter on top of the vellum side, centered on the doily, and lightly trace around the star with a pencil. Cut the star out slightly larger than the traced marking.
3. Glue the cookie cutter to doily side of the star cutout. Let dry completely.
4. Trim the doily close to the cutter.
5. Place in front of the votive candle.

Votive Gift Bags

Materials:
- Ridge Knothole Bags by Loose Ends
  Sizes
    —14" x 4" x 4" (wine bag)
    —7" x 3 1/2" x 9 1/2 " (medium vertical)
    —11" x 4" x 6 1/4" (medium horizontal)
- Caribbean Collection Papers by Loose Ends
  Colors
    —Sea Foam 5" x 10 1/2"
    —Coral 7" x 8 1/2"
    —Poupon 12" x 3 3/4"
- Corrugated Die Cuts by Paper Reflections
    —Deep Woods bears
    —Outdoors moose
- Corrugated Papers by Paper Reflections
  —Hunter 8 1/2" x 11"
- Tacky glue
- Mat knife
- Storm candle
- Two votive candle holders with candles

1. Place something sturdy inside the bag before cutting. Cut the hole only in the front of the bag.
    —Wine bag: Cut 1" up from the bottom edge (9 1/2" x 2 3/4")
    —Medium vertical: Cut 2" up from the bottom edge (5 1/8" x 5 1/8")
    —Medium horizontal: Cut 1/2" up from the bottom edge (4" x 8 1/2")
2. Glue the paper inside the opening. The top of the paper should go under the fold down at the top of the bag. For the wine bag use the poupon paper; for the vertical bag use the coral; for the horizontal bag use the sea foam paper.
3. Glue the moose die cut on the coral paper. Glue the bears on the sea foam paper. Cut the tree pattern out of the hunter green corrugated paper and glue on the poupon paper. Add a storm candle to the tall bag and place votive holders with candles in the other bags.

Tall 3-Wire Basket Candle Stand

Materials:

- Three chrome wire breadbaskets
- Wire
  —16-gauge tinned copper (20 feet), natural copper (30 feet)
  —20-gauge tinned copper (75 feet), natural copper (20 feet)
  —28-gauge brass (10 yards)
- One gross teal marble small pony beads
- Approximately 12 large green and blue flat glass marbles
- Approximately 24 dark green and blue glass marbles
- Glass and bead adhesive

Instructions:

1. Stack two baskets open end to open end matching the designs on the baskets.
2. Use the 10 lengths of 20-gauge tine wire to make five close neat wraps joining the basket tops together at the center of each of the 10 design loops on the baskets. Twist the ends of the wire together and clip off the excess. Fold the twist to the inside of the baskets.
3. Join a third basket, bottom to bottom to the top of the first two baskets. Join it in the same way as you joined the first two baskets.
4. Prepare the flat glass pieces by cutting 36" lengths of the 16-gauge wires. Alternate the following two methods as you add the glass pieces to the baskets.
   Method A—Coil one end of the wire into a tight coil. Place it on the front of the glass piece and wrap the remaining wire around it several times. Lay the glass face down and put glass glue on the back of the glass and the wire wrap. Let dry completely.
   Method B—Wrap the center of the wire around the glass piece several times. Place glass face down and put glass glue on the back of the glass and the wire wrap. Let dry completely.
   Use the remaining length of wire to attach the glass to the basket by wrapping it around the basket prongs and coiling the ends to form part of the design.
5. Add the marbles by using 1-yard pieces of assorted wires and enclosing a marble at each end on the wire by first making a tight coil and wrapping the marble in it. Make sure that the coil is tight enough to hold the marble. Attach these pieces to the basket by weaving them in and out of the basket and wrapping them around the basket prongs.
6. Thread the beads onto the 28-gauge wire. Space the beads about every 3" by twisting the wire twice after each bead is added. The result will be a 10-yard length of wire with a bead every 3". Wrap this wire around the entire basket combination.
7. Add the candle in the top basket.

Candle:
Sea glass covered candle (for directions see Chapter 9)

Two-Basket Candle

Materials:
- Two chrome wire breadbaskets
- Wire
  - —16-gauge tinned copper (20 feet), natural copper (30 feet)
  - —20-gauge tinned copper (75 feet), natural copper (20 feet)
  - —28-gauge brass (10 yards)
- One gross teal marble small pony beads
- Approximately 12 large green and blue flat glass marbles
- Approximately 24 dark green and blue glass marbles
- Glass and bead adhesive

Instructions:
1. Follow materials and directions for the Three-Basket Candleholder, but omit step three.
2. Cut a 3-yard piece of 28-gauge brass wire and add the beads as for step 6. Wrap these around the candle for this holder.

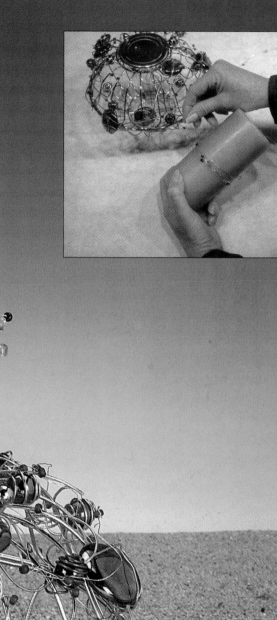

Look at what jewels I found at the local home improvement store! These pieces cost pennies and are great light reflectors. A few touches from the craft store and great conversation pieces emerge.

Vent Cap Votive Wall Sconces

Materials:

- Galvanized 4" vent cap (found at hardware store)
- 1 yard tinned copper 22-gauge wire
- Assorted small beads in blue, green, and purple
- One tuna can 2 1/2" in diameter
- Pearlized glass marble cabochons —two green and one blue
- Glass and bead adhesive
- Picture hanger (I used a small tab top glued to the back top of the vent cap)
- Green votive candle

Instructions

1. String the beads on wire. Wrap around the indentation at the front of the vent cap. Twist the wires together and hide the ends.
2. Glue the glass cabochons to the front of the tuna can.
3. Place the candle in the tuna can and place can inside the vent cap.
4. Glue picture hanger on the back top of vent cap.
5. Hang vent cap on the wall.

110

Shell Lantern Look

Materials:

- SC storm color 6" round (from hardware store)
- Aluminum duct pipe collar (from hardware store)
- Wire breadbasket
- 20" x 2 1/4" Natural Kraft Bordette by Bemiss-Jason
- Tacky glue
- 10 yards 28-gauge copper wire by Artistic Wire
- Needle-nose pliers
- Acrylic paint—shimmering silver
- Five small shells
- Five medium shells

Instructions:

1. Place the pipe collar in the storm collar, small end up. Place the basket upside down on top.
2. Cut 10 pieces of 28-gauge wire 2 yards long. Wrap the wires around the shells. Attach shells to the upside down breadbasket. Alternate the small and medium shells around the basket. Attach the small shells aimed down around the center of the basket and the medium shells upward near the top of the basket.
3. Paint the ridges of the corrugated-paper border with the silver paint. Glue it around the pipe collar under the flared section. Bend the prongs of the collar down so they stand straight out.
4. Place the candle inside the pipe color and place the basket on top.

Flexible Aluminum Duct Candle Collar

Materials:

- Flexible aluminum duct (from the hardware store)
- 6" x 6" pale green candle with three wicks
- Glass and bead adhesive
- Eight white opalescent flat marbles
- 16 green opalescent flat marbles
- 20" x 2 1/4" Natural Kraft Wavy Ridges Bordette by Bemiss-Jason
- Acrylic metallic paint—silver
- Six small conch shells

Instructions

1. Connect the ends of the duct (there are interlocking slots on duct).
2. Bend the prongs around the duct straight out.
3. Glue one white marble every third prong and fill in with two green marbles between.
4. Paint the top of the ridges on the cardboard with the silver paint. Glue it around the collar 1" from the bottom edge and evenly space the six conch shells around it.
5. Push the collar down onto the candle leaving the top of the collar even with the top of the candle.

Crackle Glass Hurricane Lamp

Materials:
- Crackle Glass small hurricane glass—3 1/2" x 8 1/2"
- 24-inch length of antiqued bead fringe
- Large tuna can with top removed
- 14" x 2" wide leaf ribbon by Loose Ends
- Glass and bead adhesive
- Clear taper holder
- 4" white molded taper candle

Instructions:
1. Glue the leaf ribbon around the can.
2. Glue bead fringe around the neck and the bottom indentation of the hurricane glass.
3. Place the can upside down with the glass taper holder and candle on top. Place the hurricane glass over the candle so that it sits on top of the can.

Balls of cording, sisal, or rope can be used to decorate a candleholder, or even be one.

Golden Yellow Classic Candle Overdipped in Blue

Materials:
- 10" golden yellow classic candle
- Blue dye
- White dipping wax
- Sisal bundle
- 1/2" PVC pipe

Instructions
1. Add blue dye to hot wax (190°).
2. Hold the candle by the bottom and dip into the wax. Do not dip the bottom 2" of the candle.
3. Dip the candle three more times in the dipping wax, each time dipping less of the candle.

Candleholder:
Displayed on a sisal bundle with PVC pipe pushed into the top half of the bundle to hold the candle.

Materials:

- Three hook ornament hangers
- Three glass votive holders
- Copper strap, 26-gauge, 3/4" wide by approximately 24"
- 22 feet of 24-gauge copper wire
- 24 black metallic beads
- Three tea light candles

Instructions:

1. Cut copper strip into three pieces approximately 8" to go around each votive as a collar.

2. Cut three 36" lengths of copper wire. Shape the collar in a circle overlapping holes at the ends. Run the wire in one hole and out the next. Add a bead every time you come back out on the out side. After all the beads have been added, keep circling the wire around the collar two more times. Secure the ends by twisting the ends together and hide inside the collar.

3. Cut the remaining wire into 12 13" strips. Use four of these strips per collar. Evenly space the four wires around the collar and push each through a hole in the copper collar and double the wire with the ends at the top. Twist the tops together and fold over the twist to form a loop. Wrap the ends around the loop neatly.

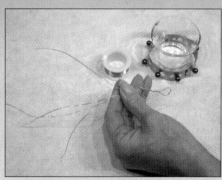

Candleholder:

Use red tea light for Christmas and yellow tea lights for anytime.

Bobeche Candles

Materials:

- 3" aluminum s/l pipe (from the hardware store)
- Scissors
- Awl or ice pick, and hammer
- 24-gauge wire
- Assorted crystal beads
  —Eight 10mm round
  —48 4mm round
  —16 12mm disc
  —Eight 13 x 6mm elongated bicone
- Needle-nose pliers
- Small, curved, cuticle scissors

Instructions

1. Patterns are given for two shapes of bobeche. Pattern A with eight points and Pattern B with rounded petal shapes. Trace pattern onto the aluminum.
2. Cut out the bobeche and cut a hole in the middle of the pattern. Punch a hole with the awl and use the small scissors to cut the hole.
3. If using pattern A, punch a hole in each point of the design close to the point. If using pattern B, punch a hole in the center of each petal very near the edge of the petal.
4. For either pattern cut eight pieces of wire approximately 8" long. Thread 1 1/2" of the wire through a 10mm round bead and fold the wire back up through the hole. Thread onto the long and short wire the following: One 4mm round, one 12mm disc (the shorter wire will soon be covered and you will be working with one wire) one bicone, one 12mm disc, and five 4mm round beads. Take the wire through one of the eight holes in the bobeches and fold the wire back over the edge and back though the small beads. Repeat this until you have one of these bead arrangements on each of the eight holes of the bobeche.
5. Place the bobeche over the candle. The bobeche's purpose is to act as a candle collar that catches the melting wax.

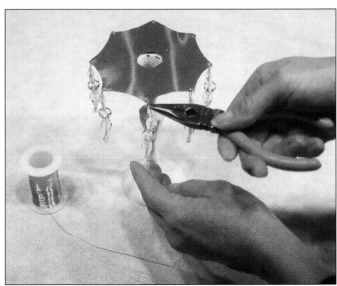

See pattern
on page 123.

Tab Top Candle Topper

Materials:

- 3" x 9" pink candle
- Pineapple chunks can with top and bottom removed
- 24 large tab tops
- 16 2" silver head pins
- Assorted E beads
- Eight colored cabochons
- Glass and bead adhesive
- Two pairs of needle-nose pliers
- Individual metal gelatin mold
- Small metal steamer
- Strawberry shake- and soft blue-colored metal paint

Instructions:

1. Using two pair of pliers at the same time, bend the 16 tabs at the center to form right angles.
2. Glue eight tab tops around the edge of the can with the tabs folded in and eight tab tops around the bottom of the can with the tabs folded out.
3. Glue eight flat tab tops around the can in between the tabs around the edges. Glue cabochons on top portion of each flat tab.
4. Thread the E beads on to each head pin. Attach two head pins to each of the outward folded tabs at the bottom of the can.
5. Place the can on top of the candle.

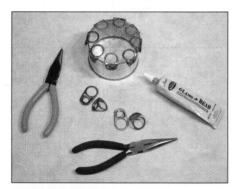

Candleholder:

1. Paint the gelatin mold with the blue paint. Use the end of a round glue stick or dowel to make dots with the pink paint.
2. Place the mold in the center of the small steamer.

Dollar store black metal candleholders were enhanced with wire and river rocks. These candleholders can be seen throughout the book.

Copper mesh (knitted mesh sleeve) from Loose Ends cut in various lengths, was placed over candleholders and wrapped with copper wire.

Picture frames and mirrors are used throughout the book as candleholders. Remove the glass and backing from the frame and add feet to make the bottoms level. Feet can be four wooden disks painted to match the frame or marble cabochons.

Wooden plaques, rustic or beveled, are perfect for candle groupings with themes such as woodland or row houses.

Upside-Down Wire Plant Hanger Candle Cover

Note: This project uses many of the same techniques that are pictures in the Tall Three-Wire Basket Candle stand.

Materials:

- Wire hanging basket by Achla Designs with hangers removed
- Assortment of sea glass (blue, light blue, green, light green, and clear)
- Assortment of glass pony beads in blues and greens
- Wire
  —12-gauge tinned copper
  —18-gauge copper
  —20-gauge tinned copper, copper, and brown
- Glass and bead adhesive
- Needle-nose pliers

Instructions

Note: This basket can be as simple or as covered with wire as you like. So, I haven't given yardages for the wire lengths, only the gauges and colors.

1. The first wire to apply is the 12-gauge tinned copper. It is the thickest and makes large swirly designs over the basket. Coil ends with the pliers and place in a free-form pattern. We worked with the basket upside down.
2. The 20- and 16-gauge wire can be used to wrap sea glass and attach them to the basket. Coil the ends of these wires as well. First, wrap a piece of sea glass with wire. Some wraps start with one of the coiled ends while others are wrapped with the center portion of a 45" length of wire. After a piece of glass is wrapped, apply glue to the back of the glass over the wires to secure. Let dry completely.
3. Weave the wire over the basket on a form design that also helps hold the previous thicker wire in place.
4. Use 45" lengths of 20-gauge wire to string beads. The beads are spaced approximately every 3". Twist the wire around the beads to keep them in place. Weave the wires over the basket and coil the ends.
5. Place the basket over the candle.

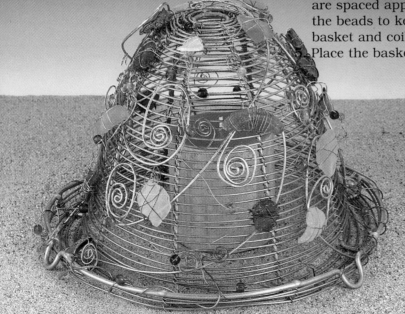

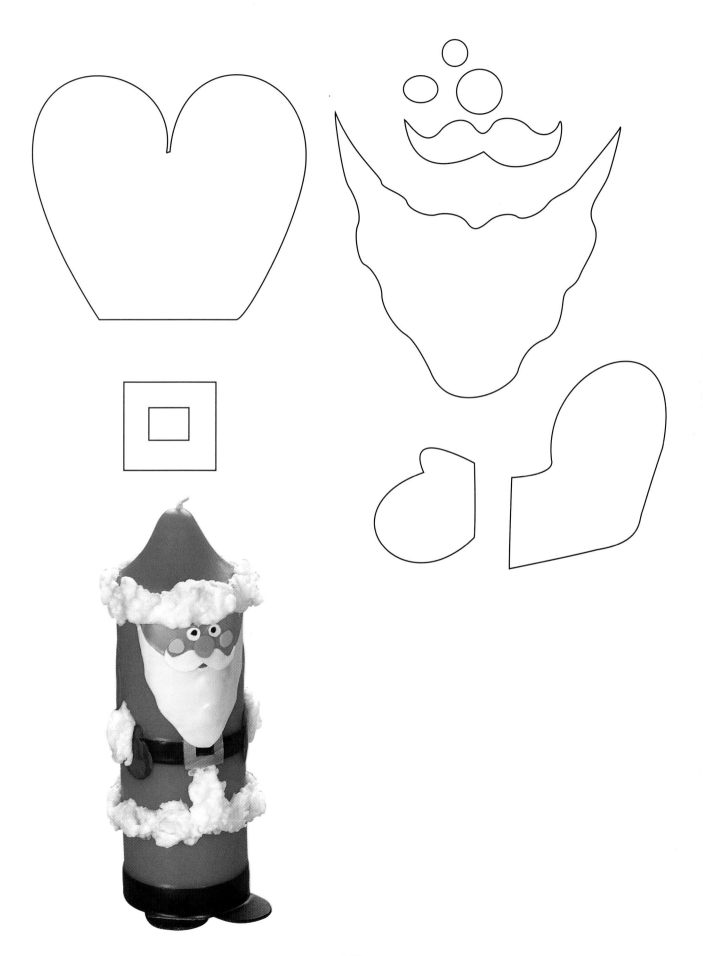

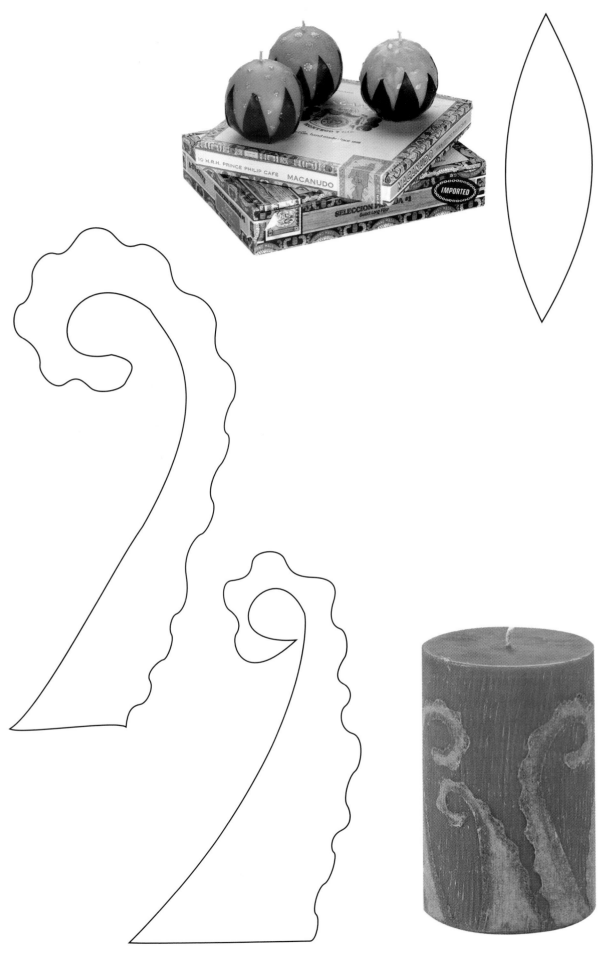

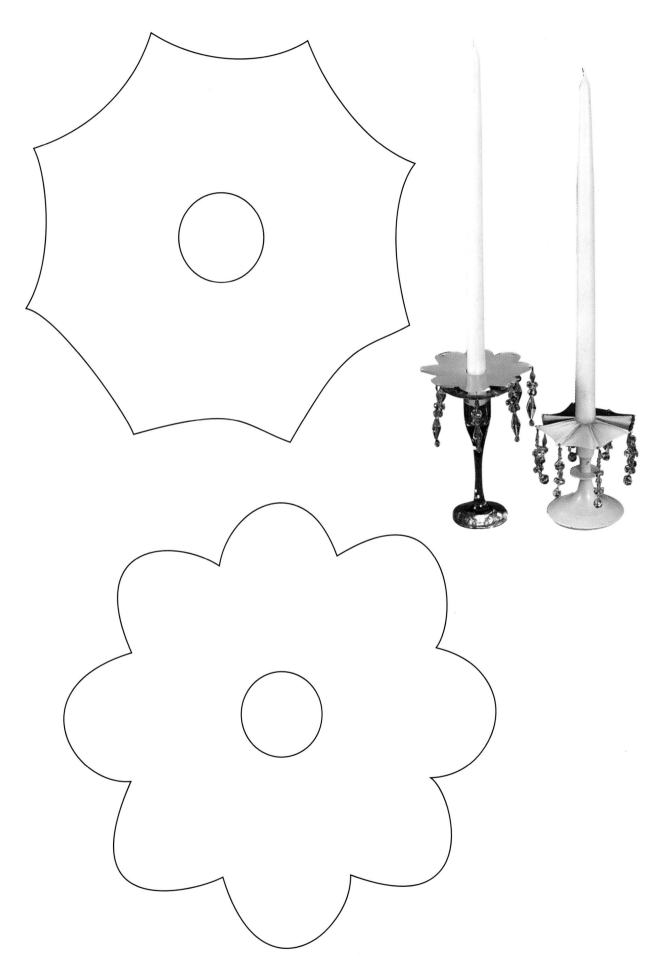

Resource Guide

Artistic Wire
1210 Harrison Avenue
LaGrange Park, IL 608526
www.artisticwire.com
All gauges and colors of wire

Colonial Candles of Cape Cod
P. O. Box 2806
Oshkosh, WI 54903
www.blythinindustries.com
Candle manufacturer

Crafter's Pick
520 Cleveland Avenue
Albany, CA 94710
800-776-7616
www.crafterspick.com
The Ultimate! Tacky Glue

Craftware
629 Boyette Road
Four Oaks, NC 27524
800-927-7714
www.craft-ware.com
email:
craftware@dockpoint.net
No-hole beads and Red Liner Industrial Strength Double-sided Adhesive

Creations By Emi
785 Sequoia Drive
Sunnyvale, CA 94086
Ecreations@aol.com
Japanese Washi paper by Aitoh Company

Creative Crystal
P. O. Box 1476
Middletown, CT 06457
www.creative-crystal.com
Swarovski Crystal tattoos

DecoArt
P.O. Box 386
Stanford, KY 40484
www.decoart.com
Americana acrylic paint, No-Prep Metal Paint, Dazzling Metallics, Faux Glazing Medium, Candle Painting Medium, and American Stains Polyurethane Varnish

DMD Industries
1205 ESI Drive
Springdale, AR 72764
www.dmdind.com
Paper Reflections line of specialty papers and diecuts

Duncan Enterprise
www.duncancrafts.com
Aleene's Platinum Bond Glass and Bead Adhesive

Emagination Crafts, Inc.
530 North York Rd
Besenville, IL 60106
www.Emaginationcrafts.com
Craft punches and decorative edged scissors

Houston Art, Inc.
10770 Moss Ridge Road
Houston, TX 77043-1175
info@houstonart.com
Gold leaf kit and varigated Black metal leaf

Jones Tones, Inc.
33865 United Drive
Pueblo, CO 81001
www.jonestones.com
White Iris Glitter Paint and Micro-fine Sprinkle on glitter

Loose Ends
P.O. Box 20310
Keizer, OR 97303
www.looseends.com
Specialty papers, trims, preserved reeds, and leaves

Lowe-Cornell, Inc.
563 Chestnut Avenue
Teaneck, NJ 07666
www.lowe-cornell.com
Paintbrushes

Papers by Catherine
11328 South Post Oak Road #108
Houston, TX 77035
Specialty papers

Sunshine Discount Crafts
P. O. Box 301
Largo, FL 33779-0301
www.Sunshinecrafts.com
Beads and cabochons from The Beadery

Therm O Web
770 Glenn Avenue
Wheeling, IL 60090
www.thermoweb.com
Peel-n-Stick double-sided adhesive

Walnut Hill Company
P. O. Box 599 Green Lane
and Wilson Avenue
Bristol, PA 19007
www.walnuthillco.com
Candle-making supplies

Yaley Enterprises
7664 Avianca Drive
Redding, CA 96002
www.yaley.com
Full range of candle making supplies and equipment

More Ideas and Projects to Create

Naturally Creative Candles
by Letty Oates

This unique art form is brought to vivid life as author Letty Oates demonstrates the immense potential of numerous natural materials in making and decorating different candles. More than 250 sharp photos reveal the results of creative candlemaking.

Softcover • 8-1/2 x 11
128 pages • 250 color photos
Item# NACC • $19.95

Year 'Round Fun
edited by Bill Stephani

Everyone who works with kids will love this book filled with inexpensive projects for every occasion! Kids will find exciting projects to make and do from January through December with the quick and easy party ideas, group activities, Bible-school projects and much more. As an added bonus, the book contains an 8-page cutout section featuring the Delta Star X7 Shuttle Lander. It really flies!

Softcover • 8-1/4 x 10-7/8
96 pages • 96 color photos
Item# YRF • $14.95

Forever Flowers
A Flower Lover's Guide to Selecting, Pressing, and Designing
by Bernice Peitzer

Make your flowers last a lifetime! This all-in-one resource includes foolproof methods for sowing, growing, gathering, pressing, storing, and designing and creating with flowers. Provides dozens of projects and ideas for beautiful, functional accents you can keep yourself or give as one-of-a-kind gifts, including pictures, jewelry, bottles, and stationery. Features step-by-step instructions, lavish full-color photos, and tried-and-true tips and techniques.

Softcover • 8-1/4 x 10-7/8
128 pages • 100 color photos
Item# PRFLO • $21.95

Essentially Candles
The Elegant Art of Candlemaking & Embellishing
by Dr. Robert McDaniel & Katie McDaniel

Create, scent, color and embellish professional looking candles at home with this full-color guide. Everyone from the beginner to the intermediate candle-maker will find it easy and rewarding to make their own candles with the step-by-step instructions for pillars, tapers, container candles, mold making and much more. Dr. Robert S. McDaniel is also the author of Essentially Soap, finalist for the 2001 Award of Excellence.

Softcover • 8-1/4 x 10-7/8
128 pages • 125 color photos
Item# ESCA • $19.95

The Complete Guide to Glues & Adhesives
by Nancy Ward & Tammy Young

In 1995, Tammy Young's The Crafter's Guide to Glues took the crafting world by storm. Now, Tammy has teamed up with Nancy Ward for this full-color follow-up that covers everything you need to know about glues and adhesives currently on the market, including their uses and applications for memory crafting, stamping, embossing, and embellishing any surface. Besides presenting the basics, like safety, there are more than 30 quick and easy step-by-step projects.

Softcover • 8-1/4 x 10-7/8
144 pages • 75 color photos
Item# CGTG2 • $19.95

Essentially Soap
The Elegant Art of Handmade Soap Making, Scenting, Coloring, & Shaping
by Dr. Robert S. McDaniel

Make "custom-made" soap with just the right scent, emollients, and eye-appeal. With Dr. Robert McDaniel's simple instructions and numerous recipes, you can make soap to match your decor, soothe your jangled nerves at the end of a hectic day, or energize you in the morning. McDaniel teaches you how to work with fragrances, skin treatments, colors, and shapes and discusses the aromatherapy benefits associated with many essential oils.

Softcover • 8-1/4 x 10-7/8
128 pages • 100 color photos
Item# SOAP • $19.95